GREEN-WOOD

DELL

BIRCH HILL

OAKLEAF AV.

BUTTERNUT HILL

AVENUE

TWILIGHT DELL

PINE HILL

DUSKY HILL

VISTA HILL

GLADE HILL

AVENUE

WOODLAND AV.

FOREST AVENUE

DUSKY VALLEY

HOLLY HILL

PINE DELL

PINE

CENTRAL AV.

CHESTNUT

FOREST RIDGE

AVENUE

MULBERRY HILL

BUTTON HILL

WOOD

LAWN AV.

LOCUST

GREENHOUGH AV.

CHERRY HILL

LAWN-GIRT HILL

SUNNY DELL

CHESTNUT HILL

AVENUE

CYPRESS AV.

CYPRESS HILL

LAWN AV.

AVENUE

HILLSIDE DELL

BAY-GROVE HILL

SYCAMORE AVENUE

MYRTLE

THE CENTRAL RIDGE

AVENUE

Y SIDE

PSE OUND

AVENUE

FERN HILL

STRAWBERRY HILL

VALLEY AV.

GLADE AV.

ASPEN HILL

LAWN

WILLOW AV.

ARBOUR WATER

SYLVAN

CHAPEL AV.

G-REEN

EVENING DELL

GREEN-WOOD

Allison Cobb

NIGHTBOAT BOOKS
NEW YORK

ISBN 978-1-937658-88-5

Design and typesetting by Janet Evans-Scanlon
Text set in Caslon
Cover Design: Mary Austin Speaker
Cover Art: Detail of map of Green-Wood Cemetery by William Lawrence and
James Smilie, 1846, courtesy of The New York Public Library

An earlier version of *Green-Wood* was published in 2010 by Factory School as part of
its Heretical Texts series.

Cataloging-in-publication data is available from the Library of Congress

Nightboat Books
New York
www.nightboat.org

FOREWORD

by Brian Teare

In his treatise *Dominion of the Dead*, scholar Robert Pogue Harrison argues that the human is defined by the humus into which we inter our dead—indeed, Vico reminds us that *humanitas* comes from *humando*, burying—and that throughout history our rituals of burial have served to maintain and protect the intimacy with the earth that makes us who we are. "Humans bury not simply to achieve closure and effect separation from the dead," he writes, "but also and above all to humanize the ground on which they build their worlds and found their histories." It's a lovely idea. It's also a profoundly anthropocentric one, in that it suggests that humans have something to offer the earth, but that the earth has value only insofar as it can be humanized or made to serve human interests. The same way we've built archives and libraries to hold the cultural memories out of which we've fashioned the western mind, we've tasked the humus to hold the dead who literally made us and the dead who figuratively make us who we are. "Teach me I am forgotten by the dead/And that the dead is by herself forgot," Ralph Waldo Emerson writes in a desperate 1831 elegy for his first wife Ellen, "And I no longer would keep terms with me." By being our memory, the dead keep individual identity alive, and the humus holds us all together at the root.

Into this set of western assumptions comes *Green-Wood*, Allison Cobb's masterly and remarkable cultural biography of Brooklyn's Green-Wood Cemetery. The leafy cemetery through which Cobb walks in the years after 9/11, during the ensuing wars in the Middle East, during her mother's cancer treatments, and during her own treatments for infertility, does indeed serve as the ground on which public and private histories are founded, the ground of her historical identity as a United States citizen in the twenty-first century. "I walk against the backdrop of war," she writes, "the toppling of the Hussein statue, declaration of end of hostilities. Continued bombings. NAMES OF DEAD in the paper." Yet Cobb complicates the traditional patriarchal view of the earth's humanizing work by contextualizing it within the high price the earth pays for its unpaid and often unsung cultural labor: "I walk by bulldozers, mowers, pesticide sprayers with yellow warning placards: KEEP OUT FOR 24 HOURS." Alert to the fact that earth's metaphysical role in western culture has for many centuries been coextensive with the role it has played in capitalism, industrialization, imperialism, and globalization, *Green-Wood* never pretends that the terms that make us human do not hold the humus hostage.

::

Though its pages of prose spliced with poetry and white space give it the surface appearance of wildness, *Green-Wood* is nonetheless closely argued and follows a compelling structural logic suggested by its subject. Like the place, whose earliest designs were intended to evoke the rural *hortus conclusus* of Eden, the book is a palimpsest under whose controlled surface a locatable original no longer lies intact. In narrating the history of ideas that led to the founding of the cemetery in 1838, *Green-Wood* sees theology in forestry, gender in etymology, philosophy in biology, and landscape design in literature, with all these disciplines also interposed between and woven into each other. In narrating a present in which the United States wages perpetual war and the author grieves both collective and individual losses, *Green-Wood* turns outward, toward the made landscape, found objects, trees, and urban animals, and locates living history in relationships with things that give weight to and elicit identity from us through co-presence. Turning away from the archives and librarians and toward the cemetery and its animals, Cobb's periodic field notes contemplate the order of things alongside things themselves on the literal ground where life and death play out.

Cobb's insistence on the equal importance of site and language to understanding our relationship to earth situates Green-Wood in the contemporary tradition of environmental writing that sprung up in the wake of *ecopoetics*, the literary journal edited and published from 2001 to 2009 by the poet-critic Jonathan Skinner. Though all ecopoetry is rooted equally in the oikos—or home—of ecology, and the poiein—or making—of poetry, postmodern ecopoetics departs from more representational iterations of environmental writing in the fierce scrutiny it brings to bear upon language itself, and especially in the way it borrows from avant-garde poetics a critical eye quick to see the anthropocentric and imperialist ideologies hidden in traditional literary language. In *Green-Wood* such criticality is played out largely through etymological research, archival work, appropriation, collage, and the resulting surprising juxtapositions, proximities that allow Cobb to reveal causal histories the culture would prefer remain hidden. For instance, the rapid deforestation of the North American continent by settlers is one of the preconditions for nineteenth-century America's love of rural cemeteries like Green-Wood, and Cobb likes to point out similar ironies about her own role as a poet:

> History makes me absurd, a poet in a cemetery, from the
> Sanskrit for "to sound," as in off-harmony. I walk
> (literally) in the footsteps of Whitman, who liked to stroll
> here.
> *a dead tree loves the fire*
>
> But every age has its ghosts, a kind of rage. The language.

For Cobb and Green-Wood, as for the environmental tradition in the United States, the twenty-first century is haunted by the nineteenth, the age of Emerson's *Nature* and the intercontinental railroad, Walt Whitman's *Leaves of Grass* and the Indian Removal Act, John Muir's conservationist activism and the oil rush of Western Pennsylvania. That century of expanding empire and quickening capitalism bequeathed our democracy its rage of contradictions, and for Cobb this is most obvious in the fact that in seizing a continent from indigenous peoples and parceling it out as private property, settlers everywhere also made it a commodity, a fact with which our literary language has often been complicit. And while on the page Cobb consistently confronts this legacy of complicity through her linguistic interventions, in the field she can't seem to help but experience a physical and affective primacy that asserts values of another order. "In spring the great egret appears," Cobb reports with pleasure, "I first see it one day as I'm rounding the corner toward Valley Water. It starts a little leap in me, unfolding into flight." This "little leap" of lyric feeling is one of *Green-Wood*'s nineteenth-century ghosts, and so is the acquisitive desire born of such sweet feeling. "I also want to possess this creature," Cobb admits, *"A kind of appetite, a trace."* In admitting to this impulse, Cobb keeps herself—and her readers—honest about the traces of nineteenth century thought, literature, and culture that remain always with us. No matter how vigilant we are, it's impossible to keep our blameless, damning appetites out of the process of making a home in the world.

::

Green-Wood was first published in 2010 by the Queens-based small press Factory School. Even then, midway through Obama's first term, it seemed like the perfect book for our global environmental situation. Though earlier this foreword called *Green-Wood* a "cultural biography of Brooklyn's Green-Wood cemetery," that's not exactly accurate. It could also be called a portrait of the Anthropocene. Or an autobiography about grief. Or an urban pastoral elegy. Or a meditation on endless war. It is all of those things, and thus it is hard to call the book any one thing without omitting a considerable portion of its many concerns.

One of the most persuasive aspects of *Green-Wood* is how, inside of an idea or site that appears contemporary or distinctly American, Cobb often discovers another time, another place. In the course of traversing Green-Wood's 478 acres, Cobb also travels to Revolution-era France and to nineteenth-century Papua New Guinea. Cobb sees these places as integral parts of the cemetery's history because of the role imperialism played in the development of Enlightenment- and Romantic-era natural sciences. Cobb is quick to point out the commodification that accompanied the acquisition of scientific knowledge—acknowledging that, indeed, objects of scientific study were often always already commodities—and *Green-Wood* argues that imperialism's global trade routes established international networks that exacted their own environmental consequences. This is an argument perhaps most widely disseminated in 2014 by Elizabeth Kolbert's Pulitzer-winning *The Sixth Extinction: An Unnatural History*, but Cobb's prescient, trenchant take reminds us that global trade also allowed ideas and scientific knowledge to flow across cultures and nations, ideas and knowledge that enabled, for instance, the composition of Emerson's *Nature*, a text whose ideals are a part of a rural cemetery like Green-Wood and of environmental politics in the United States. But Cobb's acute sense of conscience would remind us that even *Nature*—inspired as it was in part by the Cabinet of Natural History, which collected specimens from across the world—came at a high cost to those with less power and capital, to those human and non-human others empire has always treated as expendable "natural resources." It is a cost in which Cobb also implicates herself and her own book: "*hot and total ruin*," she writes, citing the poet Susan Howe, "*I sign my name here.*"

In 2018, *Green-Wood* stands as a potent, chastening reminder that our situation remains fundamentally unchanged. The grand Gothic gate at the entrance to Green-Wood remains standing. We are still at war. Globalization continues to extend capitalist ventures and deforestation deeper into remote, biodiverse regions of the Amazon and the highlands of New Guinea, among other places. Human-made climate change accelerates at an alarming pace. And though *Green-Wood* effectively immerses its reader in the global networks that characterize the Anthropocene, perhaps the most affecting work done by the text is its turn toward objects through which these networks manifest unexpected presence. Cobb often stops to focus, like Goethe and Emerson before her, "on the minuscule as a container or concentration of the whole, hoping to encounter in the small and minute not just emblems or symbols but an actual instance of the all in concentrated form." Early on in her walks through Green-Wood, Cobb begins supplementing her lists of the cemetery's tree species with lists of tributes left on the graves of the recently departed, many of whom died in 9/11 or in subsequent military operations in the Middle East. What makes these objects so moving is that they are on the one hand banal in their mass-manufactured artificiality, and on the other hand personalized and made particular by grief:

> stars and stripes pinwheel
> glow-in-the-dark angel
> muddy stuffed bunny face down near Crescent Water
> Batman action figure
> frog riding a bicycle
> Virgin of Guadalupe pen
> DADDY WE MISS YOU

In the context of *Green-Wood*, these lists are litanies: of waste and of loss, of industrialization and of death, of war casualties and mourning. In turning toward these objects, Cobb turns toward the networks that channel plastics around the world, bear soldiers across oceans and bring their broken corpses home, and unite the dead and polymers, mourners and objects, poet and notebook on the grounds of Green-Wood. Each of these found objects is like a word whose etymology Cobb is so fond of tracking down—it is first and foremost an encounter, one that is both a singular, meaningful relation in the present and a reckoning with the myriad private and public histories that brought it into specific proximity. "These are the *aspects of substance that travel across* to resurrect," Cobb writes of these gifts to the dead, "Chattering, they *enflesh* the departed from this life." It is in part by transcribing the chatter of these objects—"DEAR PAPA WE WISH WE GOT THE CHANCE TO MEET YOU card"—and in bearing witness to the enfleshment of the departed their presence enacts—"plastic baby doll wearing a cop uniform"—that Cobb decries the violent empire in whose name they died.

::

Published a year after *ecopoetics* journal put out its last issue, *Green-Wood* is both a crucial extension and a necessary complication of its project. "Let us ask what viable range of meanings the outside can have in this global age," Skinner urges in his editor's statement to the journal's first issue, "let us embrace, in the face of shifting borders, an *impure* poetics." *Green-Wood* in its marriage of archival research, amateur fieldwork, and avant-garde poetics indeed embraces generic impurity as a matter of ethics, as the only possible way of working in the global age. But *Green-Wood* complicates the legacy of ecopoetics by adding to its environmental politics not only a pointed, pervasive critique of settler colonialism, but also a feminist consciousness often either only implicit or just plain absent from many conversations about ecopoetics.

Cobb's ecofeminist politics draw upon the kinds of analysis done by ecofeminist philosophers like Val Plumwood, whose *Feminism and the Mastery of Nature* argues that all of western thought—including the political and economic spheres—is predicated on a "backgrounding" of women, people of color, and nature, who are excluded from the category of culture, collapsed into an expedient Nature, and treated as a resource upon which the world of white western men can unconditionally and endlessly draw. Backgrounding erases the dependence of western, patriarchal achievement on women, indigenous peoples, and the earth, and also pulls a thick curtain across the enormous violence done to these allegedly "natural" resources. *Green-Wood* critiques this backgrounding by bringing into the foreground the forests, humus, and people upon which western culture has tacitly relied, a reliance that has largely enslaved and destroyed them. In doing so, Cobb cracks open the meaning of ecopoetics down to its constituent roots, *oikos* + *poiein*, questioning: who defines what constitutes "home"? exactly what operations are included in "making" a home? and who and what are sacrificed in the process?

By posing such difficult ethical and philosophical questions, Cobb's ecofeminist politics demand we look again at the dead whose presence in the earth allegedly humanizes the ground upon which western culture is built. It matters, *Green-Wood* argues, whose dead we bury, whose interment we value and view as humanizing, and whose we don't. And it matters why they died. Military casualties highlight the way nationalism can hijack the afterlife. Cobb's antiwar stance does not, of course, critique those who died in the line of fire, but it does critique a war culture built on their bodies. In refusing to background these casualties, and in recording the memorials left by those who mourn their deaths, Cobb refuses to inhabit the meaning empire makes of their sacrifice. But Cobb's refusal extends to other back-grounded operations our culture nonetheless deems necessary to making itself at home. A third of the way through *Green-Wood*, the lists of tree species and memorials left in the cemetery vanish, giving way to a list of another order entirely:

Barren
Battleship
Bicep
Black Flag
Blast Off
Blitz
Breathe Easy

These are the names of pesticides in the New York State pesticide registry, which, Cobb reports, contains thirteen thousand products. These lists punctuate the remainder of *Green-Wood* as reminders of the often silent presence of pesticides in our lives, reminders that emerge from Cobb's frequent encounters with spraying on the grounds of the cemetery. Industry's endless war against the fecundity of unwanted species—a war intimately linked to propagating the agricultural fecundity on which our survival depends—reminds Cobb of her medicalized struggle with fertility, a struggle she sees as not unrelated to the omnipresence of pesticides in the food chain, toxins already proven to cause birth defects in animal species. After narrating a painful and demoralizing experience with medical imaging and subsequent treatment with Clomid, Cobb constructs the following passage:

Kaput
Kill Zone
Konk
Labyrinth
Lariat
Leisure Time

The doctor concludes that nothing is wrong with me, except, of course, for the fact that I am female, and so is my partner. Our sperm arrives by FedEx, purchased frozen from a far-away bank. (Sperm and speech intertwine—both come from the root word "to scatter.")

In the same way that it interrogates upon what ground, upon whose lives and deaths western culture makes itself at home, *Green-Wood* questions the cultural logic used to define the "natural." This passage juxtaposes manmade technologies—pesticides and artificial insemination—with the doctor's supposition that lesbianism is the root "problem," i.e., what is unnatural here. But as the presence of "Kaput" in the list preceding this scene makes clear: fertility has become a medical problem in a heteropatriarchal culture kept alive by death, a "Kill Zone," a poisonous "Labyrinth" in which both speech and sperm scatter. To be sure, Cobb's collage methods capture a necessary and compelling sense of this scattering, but her feminist commitment to critiquing the damaging norms of our culture give persuasive shape and direction to the scatter. She "discerns patterns in the seemingly unrelated episodes that *keep sending us back, inviting us to make new connections between previously unconnected phenomena.*" By pulling into the foreground the toxins that soak the ground into which we inter the dead upon which our culture founds itself, *Green-Wood* transforms a registry into a litany that joins all the litanies upon which the book is built, a haunting choral gesture that ultimately repurposes the cemetery's space of private mourning for a public mourning capacious, enraged, and inconsolable.

::

But Cobb's visionary literary work is also built on the ground of the shared cultural trauma of 9/11, a fact that's easy to forget while reading about the mourning rituals of the Kaluli people of Papua New Guinea, or orangutans in Borneo, or Emerson enraptured by the Cabinet of Natural History while France underwent a Revolution. And we *do* forget about 9/11 as we follow Cobb's walks on cemetery grounds and her forays into the reading rooms of the New York Public Library, a forgetting that has as much to do with the absorptive power of the literary arts as it does with the fact that these errands into landscape and library constitute Cobb's own attempts to escape the sensory memories of emerging from the subway and breathing in smoke from the burning towers, "a smell the brain contains/no name for."

In a way, all of *Green-Wood* is about the indirection of ontology, how when we point to origins, we encounter unexpected swerves. So Green-Wood is born of the deforestation of the North American continent, and *Green-Wood* is born of the destruction of the Twin Towers. Cobb asks us to think of the rural cemetery as a space that values the lives of trees and largely keeps deforestation *out* of its walls; similarly, she asks us to think of environmental writing as a literary tradition that actively includes the blasted landscapes of war. Like Inger Christensen's *alphabet*, which argues that human activity has altered the language of nature so fundamentally that it now includes the hydrogen bomb and the threat of our own wholesale destruction, *Green-Wood* argues that the Anthropocene has so thoroughly instrumentalized earth that its constituent elements—soil, air, water—have become weaponized by war and the industries that support it. The objects Cobb everywhere encounters on the cemetery grounds lead her back to military operations, and the emotional logic of *Green-Wood* leads us always back to grief. "I grow strange, a cry" Cobb admits at the end of the book, "and nothing else, the force that/through the darkness moves the breath."

In honor of the formal shift with which Cobb ends *Green-Wood*—a shift I will not describe so as to leave undimmed its power to surprise— I'd like to conclude this preface by stepping out from behind the curtain of objective sentences I've constructed. It should be obvious already that *Green-Wood* is a book of immense importance to me. It has been since I first read it in 2010, and my initial enthusiasm has not only survived many close readings over the past eight years, it has intensified into passionate conviction. As a feminist, queer, ecological thinker, I never cease to be moved to solidarity by *Green-Wood*'s rigorous weave of politics and thought. As a poet and critic, I never cease to be awed by its aesthetic beauty and writerly ingenuity. As a reader and teacher of nineteenth century American literature, I never cease to be impressed by its ability to both honor and critique the intellectual heritage that underwrites contemporary environmental writing in general and ecopoetics in particular. Building upon Emerson's *Nature*, *Green-Wood* extends into the present the lineage of women's environmental writing that includes Mary Austin's *The Land of Little Rain*, Annie Dillard's *Pilgrim at Tinker Creek*, Terry Tempest Williams's *Refuge*, and Rebecca Solnit's *Savage Dreams*. Drawing upon the avant-garde archival experiments of Americanist and feminist Susan Howe, it brings into this lineage of environmental writing a truly postmodern sensibility as capable of ecstatic attachment as of fracturing criticality. And situated among the work of contemporary ecofeminist poets like Brenda Hillman, Camille Dungy, and Joan Naviyuk Kane, it reminds us of the troubled ground—patriarchal settler politics—upon which all environmental writing is built. For all of these reasons, *Green-Wood* seems to me a masterpiece of the ecopoetic tradition, an important, indispensable text that challenges each of us to a reckoning: who and what have had to die for *you* to be alive in the Anthropocene?

You are about, kind Reader, to enter and explore a still yet populous Village of the Dead. Through its labyrinths of roads and footpaths—of thicket and lawn—you will need a guide. Take one that will be silent and unobtrusive, and not unintelligent.

—*Green-Wood: A Directory for Visitors,*
Nehemiah Cleaveland, 1857

Oh! if to die
Doth fill the parting soul with secret dread,
Methinks she would more willingly depart
Could she but know her consort here would rest.
Already I am half in love with Death!

—*Green-Wood Cemetery,*
Joseph Chester, 1843

oh if to die
a regular weak verb
I meant
to be hardly
words   a *quick*
ness   the place

Wait. I came to know the place by waiting. Not waiting. By standing still and also walking. I lived. From the Old Teutonic stem "to remain."

I. THE QUESTION OF A NAME

The first year I didn't set foot inside the cemetery. The still smoking hole across the water held my attention, a smell curling inside the minds of the *million-headed city*, even in sleep.

a weather breath resurrects

The second summer I thought of taking an old boyfriend from L.A. for a tour: *First Public Opening of Green-Wood's Catacombs.* We crossed the street, joined a flock of Manhattanites looking around at nowhere Brooklyn.

The catacombs turn out to be American, a filing system. The long whitewashed tunnel built into a hill exhales its blank air. We shuffle past dark little niches, each topped by a soil clogged skylight. Our flashlights find stack after stack of sealed drawers with plaques. No bodies. No bones.

Among the crowd I see Micah Garen, who will be kidnapped in Iraq while shooting a documentary about looted artifacts. Fact means not "true" but "to make." *The fact of art a trace.*

My guest also is named Micah, who prophesied the destruction of Jerusalem. This one made an anti-Bush book out of World War II propaganda posters. Later *The Washington Post* will reveal as a lie his detailed description of jumping into Panama as an Army Ranger. A fact I wore like jewelry.

On TV we will watch Micah Garen's tearful fiancé and West Village neighbors. This one will convince his captors he seeks to expose the truth about the war and they will let him go.

Lucky, "a word of mysterious origin." *Lucky,* we all said, that we came up from the subway after the planes hit but before the buildings weakened enough to collapse. And then—

Behead:

from the Old English *behéafdian*

be (with privative force) + héafod head

that rock-ribbed isle

In 1832 a *desire awoke* in Henry Evelyn Pierrepont, grandson of New York State's largest landowner. He envisioned a cemetery on Brooklyn's thickly wooded Gowanus Hills, *which he had known in the sporting days of boyhood.*

The idea was a radical one, inspired by the landmark cemeteries of Europe, such as Père Lachaise, and influenced by Mt. Auburn in Boston, the first American cemetery described as "rural." *A late word looking back through the fence.*

* * *

Fall I walk into the cemetery almost daily, between trips home to New Mexico for rounds of what is called my mother's chemotherapy, a Frankenstein of "healing" + "alchemy"

> to "chemical" transmuted
>
> from the ancient name
>
> for Egypt, *Black Earth*
>
> or Greek for *sap*
>
> > (a quick
> >
> > ness) the place

I get lost in it. Acres: 478. Interred: approximately 600,000. Plus full fall trees, among the oldest left in Brooklyn, a road enclosed in oak light. Every turn makes me take a breath. *I dilate and conspire,* so I am more like trees,
> *a net of breathing.*

My footsteps sound outside my head and in. At first I am afraid a little. Not of ghosts or seeing bodies. Maybe just of staying lost. Or of coming across someone live, a cemetery worker, who might ask me what I'm doing here.

Soon I understand, which means "to lift." The cemetery maintains its own quotidian, a rhythm. See the army of guys in green uniforms, "the greens" I think, engines strapped to backs, blowing leaves off paths. Don't fall fall. Plus constant funerals.

> *the foreign birds*

Custom held that people be buried only in the sanctified ground of churches. But epidemics of yellow fever and cholera swept the city, and the dead overflowed the churchyards. In his 1823 *Remarks on the Dangers and Duties of Sepulture,* Francis Allen describes the graveyard of downtown Manhattan's Trinity Church as *saturated with . . . flesh.*

Bones had to be dug up to make room for new bodies, and New York sometimes had to ship its dead to Boston or Philadelphia as it now does its trash: a word decayed from the sound of cut down woods. See "twig," "splinter," and "sprig."

what language did this blood once speak

I meant it

to be hardly words

not trees

* * *

In spring the great egret appears. I first see it one day as I'm rounding the corner toward Valley Water. It starts a little leap in me, unfolding into flight.

a look back, a lake

I begin to watch for it in each of the cemetery's four glacial ponds. It hunts most often in Crescent Water, a little scum-covered lake by the Gothic tomb of William Niblo, owner of Broadway's most fashionable nineteenth-century theater. He stocked the pond with goldfish, filled the grounds with *shrubbery, vines, and flowers,* and hosted parties here before he died. A discrete metal seal near the iron gate says PERPETUAL CARE. Red geraniums pool at the feet of his lion sentinels.

I sit on a wooden bench in front of Niblo. DUCTILE IRON LIBERTY BENCH NEW JERSEY reads the curved metal arm. The decorative iron scroll is stamped CHINA. The egret stands perfectly still, tilted out over the water. It has hardly a head, just eyes and beak—honed across seven million years into a living point.

Hunters nearly wiped out the egret during the nineteenth century to fulfill demand for its cascading breeding plumage on women's hats. *At her feet animals pile their fur and feathers.* In 1892, a merchant in Florida shipped 130,000 egret skins to New York.

I also want to possess this creature. *A kind of appetite, a trace.* I sit looking at it for a long time, sun buzzing down on the crown of my head, in my ears the drone of an engine pumping air into the water. This is the sound of the war against algae, ancient one-celled creature somewhere between plant and animal that feeds off light and can live almost anywhere. It spreads across tree trunks and tombstones also, giving the place on cloudy days a green sheen.

The self in this place is always late for work. I rise to go, but a cormorant pops up through the scum and flips a bright descendant of Niblo's goldfish down its gullet. Suddenly, the little pond seems fabulous, an opera. The egret stilts up toward a tree, releasing a smooth spray of shit as white as it. I see it snatch a fat dragonfly, wings sticking like a bow out of its beak.

applause, the graveyard

* * *

Not graveyard. They called them cemeteries, "a place to sleep," in imitation
of the Greeks, at least until the Resurrection.

I slept

I slept. Walking for a year. *A confined slice.* I wrote nothing, read nothing
about the place. I meant to disappear, but it kept offering its face to read,
a text with blanks and bits floating free, death

itself a fact the cemetery,

which is time and also weather,

resurrects: the HAPPY BIRTHDAY

IN HEAVEN balloon wrecked

on a branch, ABRAHAM

COTREL 1846 ALL FLESH

IS GRASS, the berry-clotted

clump of shit by the shore

of Sylvan Water, trace

of some wild animal

the crowd itself says yes

April 1834. Ralph Waldo Emerson sits in a sunny clearing in Mt. Auburn
Cemetery and experiences an ecstatic vision. His life seems *flying to pieces.*
His wife has died at age nineteen. He has left the ministry, the calling of his
father and his father before, unable to reconcile himself to the old beliefs.
He notes how the pines glitter in the light *with their innumerable green
needles* and thinks of the *great star* in its ancient passage. He sees the clouds
above him and senses the Earth beneath him and feels the harmony of all
things, himself among them.

* * *

The New York Public Library creaks. It breathes, sucking call slips through brass tubes to an invisible vault below our feet. The ancient book comes forth, encased in a cardboard envelope THIS FLAP FIRST. Book veiled for its resurrection like carved urns on tombs half draped in cloth, a sexual peeking out.

I peel back leaf after leaf. Rural cemeteries grew out of England's picturesque landscape tradition, but the Transcendentalists gave them a distinctly American character. They called on citizens to leave the *blighted city* and immerse themselves in the continent's untouched nature: *space, the air, the river, the leaf.*

The Transcendentalists fetishized the wilderness as it vanished before their eyes. The population grew ten-fold during Emerson's lifetime. Railroads stitched the frontier closed; factories bled smoke across New England. Here's globalization for you: A businessman in Boston shipped ice cut from Walden Pond to Calcutta.

By the time Emerson published *Nature* in 1836, much of the primeval New England forest was gone, the vast pine stands of the Ohio Valley about to fall to the saw. He watched mountain lions, grey wolves, bison, and elk disappear from the land.

Against this backdrop, rural cemeteries offered oases of permanence and tranquility. *O soil silence and leaf light.* They provided a sanitized version of the natural world and obscured among the *glancing foliage* the decaying human body, itself a wilderness.

they eat

As institutions, rural cemeteries reduced Transcendentalism to a prescription or breathing clean air and experiencing Romantic sentiments—loneliness, melancholy, hope. But Emerson cleaved to the wilds of the mind, *glad to the brink of fear.*

I want to go there.

* * *

In summer the news reports dead cormorants washing up on beaches from California to Washington. *A dark punctuation.* Scientists say the plankton has disappeared from warmer waters, killing off fish and leaving the birds with nothing to eat. So the Great Chain breaks upward link from link.

Following Coleridge, the poet Susan Howe calls herself a "library cormorant." Voracious. As a high school student, Howe sought books from the Widener Library at Harvard, but her father, a professor, said it would be trespassing for her to go there. *I could come with him only as far as the second-floor entrance. There I waited while he entered the guarded territory to hunt for books.*

Cormorants will live anywhere water meets land. The first summer I often see two of them fishing in Sylvan Water. The next summer, only one appears and only occasionally. It swims low in the water with its head tipped up, looking expectant, gregarious. People call them "crow-ducks, "sea turkeys," and "lawyers."

In New York, government officials oil eggs, smash nests, and shoot cormorants. The birds are flourishing because vast catfish farms off the Southeast provide a captive winter food source. They have taken over entire islands, killing everything around them with their acidic droppings. The article about the killings is titled *Balancing Act.* The story repeats itself. In the nineteenth century, hunters nearly exterminated cormorants because they competed for fish. In 2004, the government authorized shooting near fish farms. Hunters killed more than twenty thousand.

In *The Birth-Mark,* Howe reports that cormorants can be trained to fish for a keeper. Bird owners in China put a ring around the cormorant's throat to keep it from swallowing its catch. In Japan the birds are believed to bring an easy delivery—a woman should grasp a cormorant feather just as she is giving birth.

One morning, I see a lone bird standing on the shore, drying its dark wings in the sun. Howe notes that in *Paradise Lost,* Milton describes Satan perched in the Tree of Life like a cormorant. *The darkness animate.*

* * *

History makes me absurd, a poet in a cemetery, from the Sanskrit for "to sound," as in off-harmony. I walk (literally) in the footsteps of Whitman, who liked to stroll here.

a dead tree loves the fire

But every age has its ghosts, a kind of rage. The language.

Dream delivers us from dream, and there is no end to illusion, wrote Emerson.

The word comes from Latin *ludere* "to play." In the 1840s, as industrialism wrenched the culture, a wave of exuberance broke across the nation. Spiritualism swept entire towns. People heard table rappings, saw phantoms, fell down possessed by the Holy Spirit. Communes coalesced against the forces of atomization, the family withdrawing into its padded parlor.

Too late. Emerson decided not to relinquish his self-reliance, to him the ultimate frontier. He declined to join the Brook Farm commune with its intricate social structure. Instead, he made his own attempt to reorder society by inviting his servants to dinner. Maybe his voice betrayed him. They refused, and the matter slipped into silence. The silence of *Experience*.

a self is a kind of privilege, plumaged with grief

Green-Wood's founders aimed to create an Eden, and they did not fuck around with security. They promised to prohibit the entrance of all *improper persons* and to protect the rich from resurrection men, who dug up and sold bodies for medical research. Quaint. As if the mind did

>   "circle
>   a country or a place," which
>   = time, the body
>   breathing (a weather).

Think, akin to magic,
"to cause to appear." Think

thirsty constant weed

whackers, the rising

tide of grass, the force that

through the stupid

lilies drives the bone

glow from below. Think
shined-

up tendon straps.

600,000 sets of teeth lamps.

The sleepers awake, I am enclosed by iron spikes, some places razorwire.
Patrolled by security guards in cars that say K-9. I feel watched constantly.
Alive among the dead for no purpose. No grief or leaf blowing.

a lifelike picture, dear

* * *

II. THE FENCE

It is a substantial fence, eight feet high. Its horizontal bars are attached to the iron posts by a new and ingenious arrangement, adding much to its firmness. The posts themselves, unencumbered by lateral braces, are solidly fixed in large masses of concrete, extending four feet below the surface, and the result is a structure in which neatness and strength are admirably combined. By its height, by the nearness of the pales, and by the total absence of projecting ornament, this fence offers, it is believed, entire security against intrusion, while it freely admits the light and air.

a single wing, perfect in itself

(And later): *Aesthetically considered, all fences are mere intrusions, and, to a certain extent, deformities.*

I walk through fall and winter. I walk through spring. I walk against the backdrop of war, the toppling of the Saddam Hussein statue, declaration of end of hostilities. Continued bombings. NAMES OF DEAD in the paper. I walk by bulldozers, mowers, pesticide sprayers with yellow warning placards: KEEP OUT FOR 24 HOURS.

> Tree I trace
>
> from the root spelled "rot"
>
> to "worm" a proto-word
>
> subtracting wildness

let earth conceal them from our sight

A few fine old Brooklyn families—the Bennetts, Bergens, and Wyckoffs—traced their title to land on the Gowanus Hills back to their Dutch ancestors. The Great Panic of 1837 spurred them to sell out to the cemetery.

Smaller landowners refused to relinquish their holdings, a *vexation* that—along with debt on the larger parcels—kept the cemetery at first from deeding for burial *a single rood*: An echo of "wild wood" reduced to "twig" or "rod," a measuring stick, a measure of land, then the cross, an instrument of execution.

Weeping Beech

London plane tree

Cedar of Lebanon

Austrian pine

American holly, female

Yoshino cherry

Mulberry from China

> each tagged with a metal I.D. number

* * *

The weeping beech curves over the road, forming a room of green light. I stand underneath and breathe in it, really three trees clustered together. The *small-teethed* leaves seem edged with fire, shadowing leaves below. I hear a distant bus horn from the Jackie Gleason depot, and close by the sound of sparrows pecking insects from the bark.

The cemetery tree census from 1987 lists thirty-six European and American beeches and their cultivars: the cut-leaf, weeping, and purple. I have counted in one morning more than fifty. Beech trees belong to the genus *Fagus*, named for the Celtic tree god. They also are called "elephant" because of their smooth skin like a hide. This makes people want to carve them. Nearly all have graffiti, the oldest marks grown fat with the widening tree:

JULIA 1970

PETEY G.   BUBBA

7ᵀᴴ STREET CHUCK

ISH [unreadable] 1945   9/14/87 JESUS WAY

1960 RMC

[inside a little house] A.C.   TINY JOEY

D.C. [beneath a crown]

LARRY -N- JEANINE   F.G. 49ER 2001

WOLFIE + ANGEL

Ancient Saxon tribes carved runes in tablets cut from beech bark.

"Book" and "beech" split from the same root. First fence a voice.

> *Lie*
> *down ferocious feeling*

* * *

When the colonists stepped onto the shores of North America, they beheld a sight they could never have imagined in the long-cleared lands of their ancestors: A vast forest stretched as far as one could walk in every direction. Trees covered half the continent, spreading a thousand miles from the Mississippi River in the West to the Atlantic in the East, and from Maine south to the Gulf of Mexico.

Fence, stump of defense. "A thing protected or forbidden."

The Puritans came with the fear of the dark forest curled inside their minds. Their Anglo-Saxon ancestors planted the seed, but its roots drew life from the nightmares of the ancient tribes of Israel. Outside the walled Garden of Eden lay danger, the haunt of *Sathan* with his *wylye baites*.

Survival demanded war. *Every field was won by axe and fire.* Hauling off logs and prying up the stumps that gripped the earth proved a waste of precious planting time, so settlers just sowed around them, burning up the trees for fuel and fertilizer.

In fact, the forest was not the *hidious willdernes* the settlers perceived. *The ruin inside the eye.* Native societies shaped the landscape. They cleared the soil for crops, planted orchards, and burned the forest to flush out game. European settlements survived on handouts from natives, and by planting on land already cleared before them. After the Jamestown disaster, John Smith commandeered three hundred acres of cleared land at Richmond.

human seeds sprouting stones

>Catalpa
>Kentucky coffee tree
>Inkberry
>Spreading English yew
>Judas-tree
>Maidenhair
>Canada hemlock

* * *

Rune means "secret, a darkness." The Norse god Odin uncovered the knowledge of runes by piercing himself with his own sword for nine nights to the *windy world tree.*

The colonists must have taken comfort from the sight of American beeches, so like the common trees of home.

Plains tribes like the Lakota gain proximity to god by tying themselves to a sacred tree with ropes or strips of leather pierced through the skin of their chests. They pull away until the flesh rips.

> *Given to Odin*
> *myself to myself . . .*
> *I took up the runes*
> *screaming I took them*

In England the Puritans chopped down as heretical the Glastonbury hawthorn, which bloomed in winter. Believers claimed it sprouted from the staff of Joseph of Arimathea, *who craved the body of Jesus.*

"Home" in its full range and feeling belongs distinctively to English. *Lie*

> *down. Ferocious.*

The leaves of the purple beech look glossy, almost black, from a distance, but underneath they cast a cool green shadow. I circle the trunk of one and find a gash that splits the tree almost in half. Inside a pale fungus has grown in layers like lace. The trunk looks black and dead as if charred by a fire. The fungus, strangely beautiful, feels moist and airy in my fingers.

> *hot and total ruin I sign my name here*

* * *

The land on which Pierrepont envisioned Green-Wood consisted of scattered farms and pastures on a ridge of rubble left ten thousand years ago by melting glaciers. The soil proved too rocky to farm with much success, and dense stands of trees covered the slopes. For the living the ground was use-

less. A form of enduring,

the ruin or blank

inside the eye

I WILL BE SATISFIED

The area's *fine old native growth* suggested the name Green-Wood to its founders. In England, the greenwood symbolized the lawless realm of Robin Hood. But Brooklyn's leaders had in mind a *sylvan still life*, not the *frowning forest*.

As first cemetery president, the soldier and engineer David Bates Douglass set about sculpting a garden landscape. A few decades earlier, Douglass had surveyed the wilds of the Michigan Territory with its governor Lewis Cass. In hopes of luring settlers, they reported that they found *the Indians peaceful and the land promising*.

Douglass brought order to Green-Wood. He had the trees thinned and the underbrush cleared to create *the aspect of the glade rather than the thicket*. A look coming into the light:

English hawthorn

Big-leaf magnolia

American elm

Italian cypress

Black locust

Scotch pine

ancient whisper for "spear" and "spire."

* * *

First snowfall.

I follow a path scraped down to stiff grass to the grave of JOSEPH O. BEHNKE. Beside it sags a half-melted snowman, thorned branch sticking out of its back. 1958-2004, OPERATION IRAQI FREEDOM II, CHARLIE BATTERY 1/258 FIELD ARTILLERY, 95TH MILITARY POLICE BATTALION. LIVED FOR HIS FAMILY, DIED FOR GOD AND COUNTRY. A soldier carved into the stone kneels with his head down, rifle propped in one hand, helmet dangling from the other. The name MIRIAM P. is inscribed below, awaiting her dates.

word a lamp awaiting fire

In the 1940s, grave owners at Green-Wood donated the wrought iron fences around their plots as scrap for bullets and ships. Today in many places only the gates remain, connecting nothing, *an opening older than soil, an eye.*

More than a dozen condolence notes appear on the Behnke tribute site at fallenheroesmemorial.com. Specialist Kovalik ends his note: *I still feel a bit guilty though, and you know why, take care Behnke.*

The first use of the word wood to mean "insane" appears in the year 725. *They bee bitten by the wood dog the devil, and be fallen wood themselves.*

Numb with cold, I turn from Behnke's grave back toward the gate, head down against the wind. By the edge of Valley Water, I notice a stone inscribed MARTHA, with a seal for the WOMEN'S OVERSEAS SERVICE LEAGUE, half sunk in dirt. I scrape off leaves and snow with a stick to uncover the last name, EFFIE. A fat white caterpillar tucked inside the I recoils from the stick. It moves more and more slowly until it freezes in the frigid air.

I shall appear blank
a gleaming creature

* * *

The cutting went beyond the need to plant. Visitors to the New World observed that the colonists had an *unconquerable aversion to trees*. The forest connoted danger, the chaos beyond their small borders. As settlements grew, people *cut away all before them without mercy*, clearing every tree in sight.

Eventually, pioneers discovered the use of gunpowder to blast even the tree trunks out of the earth. In his travels, Alexis de Tocqueville noted the Americans saw nothing unusual in this *incredible destruction* transforming the landscape.

insurge, a spring rising up

Zelkova

False cypress

Horse chestnut

Red oak

Larch

Gingko

Elderberry

Winged Euonymus

Trees absorb whatever the soil takes up. In the Great Bear Rainforest of British Columbia, where salmon come to spawn and die, fish-derived nutrients can be measured at the top of a 250-foot spruce.

Anglo-Saxons believed the roots of the yew would find the mouths of the dead and stop them from speaking. *Chill / Fingers of yew be curled / Down on us* (T.S. Eliot). The bark of the Pacific yew contains a toxin that stops the division of cells in cancer. Several hundred-year-old trees are required to treat each patient. Clear-cutting has decimated yews in the Pacific Northwest, so researchers synthesized the drug Taxol® from cultivated yews of other species.

In Emerson's poem "Woodnotes II," a pine tree addresses the poet:
So waved the pine-tree through my thought
And fanned the dreams it never brought.

* * *

April 1838. The New York state legislature votes to recognize Green-Wood as a *body corporate* with the right to hold two hundred acres. In May, U.S. troops begin rounding up Cherokees in Georgia and marching them west of the Mississippi.

From Concord, Emerson raged against Indian Removal. In an impassioned letter to President Van Buren, he warned that the *crime* of forcing the Cherokees to leave their lands would make *the name of this nation . . . stink to the world.*

In the end, the government drove more than eighty thousand Cherokees, Chickasaws, Choctaws, Creeks, and Seminoles to "Indian territory." On the Trail of Tears, approximately one-quarter of the Cherokees died.

> *Every fact is a new*
> *word,* a god
> of mercurial mind:

The numbers shift and slide. Official recorders don't keep track of worth-
less lives.

> *the ruin inside the eye*

Emerson later lamented that in New England, Indians had become *a picturesque antiquity.* But not all indigenous people had been killed or driven from the North. In his eulogy for Thoreau, Emerson points out that his friend traveled to Maine to learn about the tribes there, and he visited with a group of Penobscots that sometimes camped in Concord. Emerson didn't expect Thoreau to learn much from the local natives: *he well knew that asking questions of Indians is like catechizing beavers and rabbits.*

Distant tribes were easier to romanticize. To survive, the Cherokee had assimilated. They formed a republic with a bicameral legislature and European judicial system. White blood pulsed in the veins of many Cherokee leaders. Some owned plantations and slaves. Emerson praised the *painful labors of these red men to redeem their own race from the doom of eternal inferiority.*

Emerson planted apple trees on Algonquian land and dreamed he ate the world.

> *our days demand fire*

* * *

Across the road from the bust of Horace Greeley, I find seven graves laid into the hillside in a row:

VERNON PAUL CHERRY FOREVER LOVED OCT. 10, 1951 TO SEPT. 11, 2001. The hinged metal oval opens to reveal a portrait of a black man in uniform, eyes closed, singing into a microphone.

> *empty. animal air.   the ear*
> *cannot help but stare*

PETER ANTHONY VEGA JUNE 15, 1965 TO SEPT. 11, 2001.
Boy-sized football shoulder pads.

JOSEPH AGNELLO BELOVED HUSBAND, FATHER AND SON OCT. 10, 1965 TO SEPT. 11, 2001.

LAWRENCE G. VELING OCT. 29, 1956 TO SEPT. 11, 2001. ENGINE CO. 235.

KARL H. JOSEPH ALWAYS IN OUR HEARTS NOV. 5, 1975 TO SEPT. 11, 2001.

CAPT. VINCENT E. BRUNTON LADDER 105 JAN. 2, 1958 TO SEPT. 11, 2001.
A faded can of Bud.

UHURU GONJA HOUSTON AUG. 22, 1969 TO SEPT. 11, 2001.
WTC PORT AUTHORITY POLICE 811. HUSBAND, FATHER, SON, AND BROTHER

A green pulls up in a truck and asks if I'm all right. Sunglasses and moustache.

Yes, I say. "So be it."

* * *

After a year, the doctors declare the cancer gone from my mother's body, *a belfry whose sad voice is seldom hushed.* This is where it begins. Before I didn't want words. But I'm cursed, I bring a notebook, binoculars. It will be "reportage" I think, a thing to carry back.

SEPARATED FROM THIS LIFE

A K-9 guard stops. He tells me not to sit in the grass (from "that which grows"). He says, *They don't want you to sit in the grass.*

"They" I find in the Rose Main Reading Room at the public library. Nehemiah Cleaveland, Green-Wood enthusiast and original historian, sprung from the root of "to see." I get ensnared by him also, that name, *Nehemiah*, open-mouthed.

Cleaveland came from a line of preachers, doctors, and pioneers, but he gave himself to the book. He served as headmaster of a *very pleasant* Brooklyn School for Young Ladies.

a slab laid on the ground looks low, and mean

Although he held no official position with the cemetery, Cleaveland at some point became obsessed. He left teaching in 1848 and devoted the last thirty years of his life to Green-Wood. He published a number of detailed guidebooks, an exhaustive history, and *Hints* on gravesite etiquette: *We reverence a mother's grief. We can look, but with pity, even on its excess.*

Pagoda tree

Tupelo

Trumpet creeper

Willow

Peony

Persimmon

the Rosebay rhododendron

* * *

The wilderness threatened to swallow the New England Puritans. Cleaveland described the state of mind of the settlers, surrounded by a forest filled with *Indians, so swift, so stealthy, and so revengeful, it was not possible ever, or anywhere, to feel secure.*

But danger also lurked within. *Sensuality, Drunkenness, and whorish Fashions* betrayed a *Heathenisme* that left the English no different from the *vile Indians.*

a sort of scorched awake

The republic also required restraint. Where men agree to govern themselves, order depends on private virtue. The Founders understood the word as masculine from its Latin root: "virility, strength, endurance." John Adams wrote that human passions were a weakness of representative government. The individual must rule himself *under the monarch of reason and conscience.*

In his 2005 inaugural address, George W. Bush echoed this sentiment: *In America's ideal of freedom, the public interest depends on private character . . . Self-government relies, in the end, on the governing of the self.*

In this vision, freedom and private property come as twin blessings. Since the Puritans came to America, religion and profit had *jumped together.* But riches had to be kept in check, or they could fuel *vicious and luxurious and effeminate Appetites.* The Founders obsessed over the fall of Rome, rotted by its own corruption. They worried that Americans, with their love of British fineries, might follow, *wallowing for ever in one continual puddle of voluptuousness.*

Cleaveland inherited the Puritan spirit. He praised the pilgrims for *the greatness of their self-denial,—the grandeur of their stern resolve.* The *incessant conflict* faced by the first settlers *had little tendency to make them scholars,* he wrote, *but it* did *make them* men.

His cemetery guidebooks offer occasion for a series of mini-sermons on the need for masculine restraint, even in death:

> The headstone covered in marble roses, the pillar stuck all over with wreaths and emblems, demand and receive the same admiration as we bestow on her, who endeavors to compensate for want of beauty, by overlaying her person with jewelry, and lace, and flowers, and flounces.

* * *

Today I find an airplane part in the cemetery. A metal tag glints from dirt beneath the hedges near Sylvan Water.

BRITISH AEROSPACE

AIRBUS TAIL CONE

MFG. DATE MAR 1999 MFR. K0999

PART NO. D58555726001008

The first five digits match my Social Security number. From *nem* the root of "divide": *The horse of disaster rides inside a blank sky.*

* * *

I begin making lists of all the *juicy intervals* I encounter. These are the *aspects of substance that travel across* to resurrect. Chattering, they *enflesh* the departed from this life:

stars and stripes pinwheel

glow-in-the-dark angel

muddy stuffed bunny face down near Crescent Water

Batman action figure

frog riding a bicycle

Virgin of Guadalupe pen

DADDY WE MISS YOU pumpkin

* * *

Cleaveland and Emerson both descended from powerful New England families. Both their grandfathers served as ministers in the Revolutionary Army. The long-time cleric at Topsfield, Massachusetts, where Cleaveland was born, was Emerson's great granduncle John. Both taught school and studied theology. As public intellectuals, both lectured on the lyceum circuit.

Cleaveland admired Emerson. He called him *the beautiful writer, and the eloquent apostle of Transcendental philosophy.* But Emerson charted the edges of thought; Cleaveland clung to institutions. He spent much of his life in rural Byfield Parish north of Boston as headmaster of the Dummer Academy, a charity boarding school for boys. (Cleaveland scoffed at the modern title "preceptor." He preferred master—*a strong, old word.*)

who grows ashamed before the blown rose

Although he regarded with suspicion the merely beautiful, Cleaveland admired the ornate entrance gate to Green-Wood. He understood its neo-Gothic architectural style as inherently Christian—*entwined with ideas of reverence and worship. . . . Keep it in your eye, until you see and feel the richness of the tracery.*

Champions of Gothic architecture saw in its soaring structures the spirit of tree groves sacred to the ancient tribes of Europe. Stained glass mimicked the effect of sunlight through leaves.

The first buildings were trees wrote the ancient Roman architect Vitruvius, but the best buildings echo the body. He advised against cutting trees for timber in spring, when they are *pregnant . . . empty and swelled out* from the effort of putting forth leaves and fruit. *Hence slaves about to be sold are not warranted sound if they be pregnant.*

Pupil in Latin means "little-girl doll": the tiny image one sees of oneself in another's eyes.

I read Vitruvius on a web site of the University of Chicago. In the background floats a pale image of the World Trade Center towers.

⊞ ⊞ ✶

Sweet gum
Crab apple
Red maple
Ash
Tulip tree
Sassafras
Little-leaf linden

Wood drove the nation's industrialization. Wood powered the steam engines, fueled the iron smelters, and fed the railroad. Between 1800 and 1900, the nation burned its forests into the atmosphere, then turned to digging fossil forests from the ground.

With increasing rapacity, loggers moved across the continent. First they cut out the hardwood and pine forests of New York and New England. Then they felled the white pine of the Lake States, then the longleaf and loblolly pine of the Southeast. Finally, they reached the sequoias and bristlecone pines of California, among the largest and oldest trees on earth.

All that ever lived about them cling to them, Emerson said about trees.

At the consecration of Sleepy Hollow, the rural cemetery in Concord, Emerson called for an arboretum of American trees *so that every child may be shown growing, side by side, the eleven oaks of Massachusetts; and the twenty willows; the beech, which we have allowed to die out of the eastern counties; and here the vast firs of California and Oregon.*

Historian Silvia Federici notes that the Europeans who colonized the Americas brought back the promise of an endless supply of native labor, which echoed their descriptions of the infinite forest.

You can almost see behind these pines the Indian with bow and arrow lurking.

When Nor'easters blew in, Whitman liked to put on a waterproof coat and lie under his *great oak, five feet thick* watching the leaves drip and the *clouds roll in furious silence.* On his sixtieth birthday, Whitman dreamed his favorite trees came walking toward him.

* * *

In winter I first see the red-tailed hawk, startling me startling it into flight. A huge bird with broad, sand-colored wings, it moves with steady flaps among the trees. It opens something up in me, a little river. One day I find three of them perched together at the top of a bare magnolia. I stand at the edge of myself in the sun, stupidly, just looking.

The star hawk, I learn, is named Big Mama. *Anything is a mirror.* A pale female larger than all the others, she is called "docile," which means unafraid of people. One morning I come within yards of her, perched in pine shadow atop a granite urn. Territorial mockingbirds bombard her then flit away fast—peck and flap, peck and flap. She flinches a bit, not moving, one yellow eye turned toward me.

In spring Joe Borker, birdwatcher, finds a female hawk floating in Dell Water. The pair that nests in the towering oak by the mausoleum failed to reproduce last year, and no one knows if the male will abandon the nest or find a new mate.

I stand on Ocean Hill and look through binoculars at the pile of dark twigs near the crown of the old tree. In 1873, Cleaveland described this vista:

> The eye ranges from Flatbush, through New Utrecht to the sea, over a level tract of farming land, charmingly variegated with wood, meadow, and green of every tint and shade, and dotted all the way with white cottage homes . . . Beyond this . . . lies the Ocean, with bays, inlets, and islands, with smoke-wreathed steamers, snow-white sails, and everything, indeed, that makes it now grand, now lovely, always interesting.

I see the glint of cars on Fort Hamilton Parkway, hazy buildings, a line of smog, and in the distance Coney Island's spindly Parachute Drop. The nest when I come to look is always empty.

* * *

Cattail

Clematis

Cotoneaster

Pear

Matrimony vine

Virginia creeper

The logging continued unchecked until settlers began to notice that the loss of forest harmed the soil. Trees *stopped the land from coming apart.*

I think that I shall never see
a poem as lovely as a tree.

A tree whose hungry mouth is prest
against the sweet earth's flowing breast.

Soon after Green-Wood opened its gates, a consciousness about the forest arose. Some, *who claimed to be arbiters of taste,* opposed cutting down the trees. The charismatic minister Henry Ward Beecher, whose bones rest in Green-Wood, expressed the progressive view: *To the great tree-loving fraternity we belong. We love trees with universal and unfeigned love, and all things that do grow under them, or around them—the whole leaf and root tribe!*

Cleaveland is defensive about the clearing and wary of the *idle rage for planting.* He devotes an entire section of the Green-Wood history to trees. TOO MUCH SHADE—AN EVIL TO BE CHECKED:

> Formerly, the forest stood in the way. The great object was to clear up the country, and hence our fathers swept off the trees with unsparing hand. Now we go to the other extreme . . . Clearly this is wrong, unless it can be shown that a stagnant atmosphere—that shade, and dampness, and mouldiness, and decay—with whole armies of bugs and caterpillars—are promotive of cheerfulness and conducive to health.

> If the luxury of planting must be indulged, let the trees selected be those of a dwarfish type, and of attenuated foliage; and, let even these be 'few and far between.'

* * *

heart pillow wrapped in a plastic grocery bag
smiling cop with one arm broken off
Hello Kitty sticker that says SMARTFIT
knock-kneed mummy with green teeth
Puerto Rican flag fuzzy dice
wrestling Dalmatian puppies figurine
MERRY CHRISTMAS IN HEAVEN ribbon

* * *

In summer I find the bloated carcass of a raccoon floating upside down in Crescent Water. Tiny fish surround it, maybe feeding off it. Half its fur is gone, the rest a grayish white mat, a few sharp teeth visible. It may have fallen in while fishing for snails—a trail of silver shells lies scattered on the shore. One leg, worn down to brownish bone, is tucked beneath its chin. The skin, stretched taut, is white and brown flecked.

Raccoons are a scourge of the cemetery. They dig burrows throughout the grounds, eat beech nuts and berries, and deposit their seeded droppings. In winter, they leave tiny handprints across the frozen crust. One day I see a bright-eyed baby poke its head from a hollow high up in an oak.

They see with their fingers. For more than two million years raccoons have been developing their sense of touch. Scientists studied their brains and found a large portion devoted to processing this sensation. They can create a picture of their surroundings through touch that is as detailed as our visual record.

The word "raccoon" is Algonquian. John Smith rendered it *raugroughcum*. The *New York Times* says Virginian Algonquian is one of the few languages to put more emphasis on listener than speaker. The verbs change inflection according to the addressee.

* * *

Green-Wood's Battle Hill rises to the highest point in Brooklyn. The climb unfolds sweeping views of New York harbor, a throb of blue between freeway and sky. To the north, the grey financial district skyline shows it hole, a myth of twins

who fought the gods
and fell in fire
to lead armies

the fruit of all rivers

The first major engagement of the Revolution erupted across this ground. On August 27, 1776, American snipers hidden in the trees took aim at British officers on the road below. In the end, more than nine thousand British soldiers surrounded a few thousand regulars. Brooklyn residents uncovered bones from this battle for years.

In spring 2006, construction workers found seven hundred bone fragments on the roof of the Deutsche Bank building. For years the black-shrouded tower loomed over the ruins of the World Trade Center, while the bank fought a *bitter battle* with the city and its insurers over who should pay to take it down.

Green-Wood also had to fight for Battle Hill. One landowner, a Monsieur Chagot, made himself an *irritating thorn* in the side of Green-Wood by refusing to sell for twenty-five years as graves encircled his fields. Cleaveland accuses Chagot of *avarice, ignorance, and obstinacy combined.* But he ends with a paean to the American system: *far better that the rights of property as guaranteed by law should sometimes be abused by its possessors, than that they should ever be violated by others . . .*

In the end, New York gave Deutsche Bank $90 million for its building. *The private sector was unable to create a solution* explained state officials.

On September 11, Deutsche Bank switched to backup systems in Dublin to conduct $300 billion worth of currency trades. According to the *London Times* this helped keep the world economy going.

As for the bones themselves, whether in atmosphere or soil, they will endure many centuries.

* * *

metal butterfly with socks on cuddling a caterpillar
YOU DIRTY X#@!* BUT I STILL LOVE YOU rock
plastic skeleton torn in two
Budweiser can made of spraypainted daisies stuck in Styrofoam
doll with yellow yarn hair and HAPPINESS BABY CLUB diaper
KISS ME I'M IRISH banner

* * *

I find a second hawk floating face down in Dell Water. Its wings are half-spread and its tail, partly submerged, looks black instead of red. No one knows what kills the hawks or why they die in the same place. It could be poisoned rats from the Wendy's across the street.

The birdwatchers decide I have found the Green-Wood male. For weeks it seems the nest might be abandoned, but then Big Mama returns to her place of birth with "Shit Face," a small, brown-streaked hawk from Prospect Park.

Big Mama spends May in the nest. Every day we come to look. In the first week of June, a single fluffy nestling appears, later than usual. It stays pushed up close to the bulk of Big Mama. One cold and rainy day it has even wedged itself underneath her.

By the end of June, Baby Huey is up on the edge of the nest. "Big Red" suggest some workers, but Baby Huey sticks. Its head seems small and fuzzy compared to its substantial body. It spreads its wings, startlingly wide and dark, and jumps on powerful legs still covered in fluff. Because of its size, the birdwatchers guess female.

In the final days of the month, Baby leaves the nest. Unable to hunt yet on her own, she hangs around Ocean Hill, perched even in driving rain on top of crumbling marble. One day I scare her off MANNING, ALFRED C. 1825-1891 AND ELIZABETH PRICE HIS WIFE. She leaves behind a mostly eaten squirrel. Its face, with closed eyes, points toward me, a blanket of flies shifting across it. One pink leg bone sticks straight up. Baby watches from a nearby tree making little whines of distress. A hot meat smell drifts toward me.

'TIS BUT THE CASKET THAT LIES HERE.
THE GEM THAT FILLED IT SPARKLES YET.

* * *

For the Puritans, outright ownership of land was a relatively new concept. Until enclosures became widespread in England, land was not held absolutely but shared through a system of interlocking rights, in which the king owned everything.

The Pilgrims at Plymouth established common field labor based on ancient English tradition. But the system caused unrest among settlers facing starvation, who *did repine that they should spend their time & streingth to worke for other mens wives.* Then *God in his wisdome* delivered to Governor William Bradford a solution: private plots. The fact that each family had to *trust to them selves for food,* he wrote, made *all hands very industrious.*

The concept became the founding principle of the nation. Property ownership served as a mark of personal virtue: One who could subdue the wilderness could also govern the self. Twelve of the thirteen original states decreed that only property owners could vote.

one word, sired in the throat

Green-Wood's trustees applied the same concept to the cemetery. They sold lots for $100 to individuals *and their successors in ownership, exclusively and forever.* They hoped that private ownership would preserve this piece of green Earth from the *disgusting spectacle* of graves all over the city being dug up for buildings and streets.

The thousands of small owners, however, made Green-Wood essentially common ground, and not all of them displayed the restraint appropriate to a republic. This fact vexed Cleaveland no end. His writing brims with exhortations on everything from proper memorials (the obelisk he dismissed as an *ambitious chimney*) to appropriate tombstone mementoes: *The grave is no place for toys, and as to the artificial flowers, they belong to Canal-street.*

But Cleaveland liked some things wild. In a fit of enthusiasm, he commends to visitors the newly purchased southeast section of the cemetery, one hundred acres still thick with trees:

> It is strictly a forest path—a ride in the woods . . . you find yourself hedged in by an impenetrable fence of stems and verdure. Hither, tired denizen of the city—poor mortal, weary of man, and strife, and business, and pleasure, and care,—hither come! Enjoy this stillness—enjoy the seclusion—enjoy yourself!

* * *

Cleaveland would appreciate the day I choose to find his grave. It is sparkling fall, with a strong wind blowing the smog away. I stop in a grove of giant tulip trees and watch them sway, leaves showering down around me.

Whitman imagined the tulip tree the *Apollo of the woods—tall and graceful.* Its leaves are the size of my palm, pocked with brown chewed-out spots. The *Audubon Field Guide* calls these the tallest and most beautiful of eastern hardwoods. *Trees with massive trunks existed in the primeval forests but were cut for the valuable wood. Pioneers hollowed out a single log to make a long, lightweight canoe.* The tulip tree holds the husks of its blooms all winter. They make the dark branches seem to glow.

The word "forest" itself forms a fence. In the eleventh century, William the Conqueror enclosed the English woods as a royal hunting preserve. Forest law meted out harsh punishments for trespass: Those caught with hands red from the blood of the king's deer could have their eyes gouged out and their testicles cut off.

But landless peasants had little choice. They continued to carve a subsistence from England's woods and common fields for seven hundred years, until the Enclosure Acts privatized most of the "wastes."

> *where light makes, even*
> *us, its face*

The eighteenth-century jurist William Blackstone wrote the authoritative interpretation of English common law. His writings mark the trail to the U.S. Constitution. He asserted that private property rights served as a fence, even where none existed: *an ideal, inviolable boundary, existing only in the contemplation of law.*

Thomas Jefferson imposed this vision of ownership across the as-yet unsettled continent. He chaired the committee of Congress that in 1785 passed the Land Ordinance. It divided the entire Northwest Territory into townships of 36-square miles, subdivided into 640-acre parcels for sale.

The grid system erected countless invisible barriers across the vast landscape, forcing native societies that had lived on the land for centuries to contemplate a new reality.

> (From "temple," to mark out a sacred space
> for observing the will of the gods.)

* * *

Green-Wood is running out of ground for burial. To gain more space, workers dig up a road near the cluster of weeping beeches. The center tree is dying. It leafs late, putting out a few deformed growths, and stays mostly bare all summer.

One day in place of the road I find a hole. It is at least fifteen feet deep and very wide. Next to it lies a large heap of dirt covered with AstroTurf—the usual practice for funerals. I look down into the hole, inhaling the cool breath of soil. Roots wave from the walls like coral. Inside lies a pinkish metal coffin with a smattering of dirt and three red carnations on top.

The next day there is only a level square of ground, slightly darker than the surrounding earth. Soon other coffins populate this spot. The most decorated stone, visible from the road by its mounds of colorful fake flowers, belongs to SERGEANT MANNY HORNEDO BELOVED SON, HUSBAND AND FATHER BORN MARCH 17, 1978 DIED IRAQ JUNE 28, 2005 OPERATION IRAQI FREEDOM II.

A portrait laser-engraved in the shining black granite depicts a man with expressive lips and a crew cut. A slightly faded basketball rests by a SON sign bordered with plastic purple roses. A toy bird on a stick, its wings on springs, sways slightly in the breeze. Two American flags are planted in the dirt. On the white stripes of one, written in red marker: I NEVER FORGET YOU ALWAYS IN MY HEART! SGT. ANGEL RIVERA. On top of the stone sits an upside down glass column etched with a cross and praying hands. I turn it over.

* * *

Sumac
Sweetbay
Wisteria
Fir
Hickory
Hornbeam
Hydrangea

On Sept. 14, 2001, *Chicago Sun-Times* movie critic Roger Ebert called for the World Trade Center site to be filled with trees and grass. *Give it no name*, he wrote.

Sherwin Nuland, the Yale surgeon who wrote *How We Die*, proposed a meditative garden at the site in words that match nineteenth-century descriptions of the role of rural cemeteries. It should be, he said, *a place where we can free ourselves from the hurly-burly of our daily lives, a garden of thought and retreat in the midst of the towering city.*

But the sixteen acres held in the gaze of millions instantly had a new name. *The tomb unfolding zero.* In the strange afterimage of the market, it still comprised some of the most valuable real estate on earth. The Port Authority wanted to keep flowing the $100 million in annual rent it received off the site. It vowed to replace all the vanished office space.

the fence itself is a blindness. a blank.

Beginning in 1846, Emerson planted a hundred fruit trees on his land. He accepted *the inevitability of private property and the inequality of means*, says his biographer Robert Richardson.

The idea of common fields evokes a mythic English past that may never have existed says the literary critic Rachel Crawford. The notion of communal land shared in harmony depends on the fence to hold it at a distance, *a landscape of loss* bathed in nostalgia.

The sixteenth-century writer Thomas Lodge depicted rioting commoners as a source of chaos that threatened to turn civilized life upside down, convincing displaced farmers that *warre is a good tree, and bringeth forth good fruit.*

* * *

half-burnt cigarette tucked under #1 MOM rock
miniature Dominican Republic maracas
I LOVE EWE snow globe with lambs lying down
lawn gnome holding an apple (red)
solar-powered cherub, wings flapping back and forth
plastic bunny with most of its fur missing
porcelain HAVE A MAGICAL CHRISTMAS bell

* * *

By 1920, one of the largest forests ever to grow on the planet was gone: 700 million acres—about eighty percent of the original tree cover—had been cut down.

Industrial technologies widened the scope of destruction. Railroads allowed loggers to penetrate deeper into the woods. Loading machines dragged massive trees to the rails, knocking down everything in their path and scraping off the soil. This left wastelands where nothing could grow back.

Silk tree
Sugar maple
Japanese bamboo
Yellowwood
Walnut
Scholar tree
Viburnum

The word "lumber" itself means something useless, an obstacle. It first appeared as a term to describe timber cut for market in Massachusetts, 1662.

Benjamin Franklin believed the increase of European whites implied by the cutting of trees would make the country lovely. *We are Scouring our Planet, by clearing America of Woods, and so making this Side of our globe reflect a brighter Light to the Eyes of the Inhabitants of Mars or Venus.*

The Indian *is perhaps destined to disappear with the forest,* mused Lewis Cass, pioneer partner of David Bates Douglass, and the man in charge of Indian Removal. He drew his justification for the policy from Genesis: Native Americans merely *traversed* the land without *subduing* it. *The human race could not well subsist, or greatly multiply, if rude tribes . . . were entitled to claim and retain all the boundless forest through which they might wander.*

In de Tocqueville's imagination, the forests of America were so thick they were like a blinding mist.

The British historical geographer Michael Williams says the trees were like air to the early settlers—so abundant they didn't even see them.

* * *

Arbor-Vitae

Crabapple

Deutzia

Haw

Golden-rain tree

Grape-Holly

Black gum

Emerson drew inspiration for his orchard from Andrew Jackson Downing, who brought landscape gardening to America. Downing felt that although the nation had vanquished its wilderness, what replaced it—the scarred frontier or the teeming city—left little to create a feeling of fondness for the land.

Downing took his ideas from the English fad for romantic gardens that began a century earlier. The movement rejected as elitist the formal plantings of the old aristocracy, emphasizing instead the "genius of the place"—the natural characteristics inherent in the landscape.

The movement also depended on the Enclosure Acts, which created large estates under the control of a single owner. The historian Gordon Mingay says that few villages actually were razed to create landscape parks. But Elizabeth Barlow Rogers points out that iconic gardens like Stowe and Castle Howard required sweeping away whole houses, pastures, and farms.

hunters, hoping their darling

The Pilgrims at Plymouth took over the remains of Patuxent, a village filled with the bones of natives wiped out by disease. In the first three months, half the settlers died, sometimes two or three a day. Emerson's ancestors at Concord also took over a deserted native town. They dug their first shelters into the ground.

What is the Earth itself but a surface scooped into nooks and caves of slumber? asked Emerson.

Walt Whitman: *What is this separate Nature so unnatural?*
What is this earth to our affections? (unloving earth, without a throb to
     answer ours,
Cold earth, the place of graves.)

* * *

I stand at the edge of Crescent Water, muggy air clinging to my skin. The pond is cloaked in duckweed and clotted with plastic bags. A rotten smell rises from the water. Bubbles break the surface everywhere, making audible pops.

A large rock protrudes from the muck. It blinks. Only then do I see the lovely striated iris *(the lattice line of everything)* and the tiny, almost delicate nostrils in a fearsomely hooked beak.

Emerson considered the snapping turtle an emblem of courage. He wrote that it will keep its jaws clamped around a stick even after its head has been cut off and that embryos in broken eggs bite fiercely *before yet their eyes are open*. He doesn't say how he came to know these facts.

The turtle sinks its head back under, and something farther out roils the water. Another snapper. I trace its progress by the rising bubbles. It surfaces right at my feet, a monster, dark and shiny. I glimpse a massive foot, webbed and clawed, an edge of shell, and it's gone.

The feeling of slightly startled amazement ebbs out of me. I want to shout and wave to the weed-whacking guy across the way, but desire won't translate to gesture. I remember I don't really belong here, and I turn back toward the trees.

* * *

Private property rests at the heart of the U.S. Constitution. In the economic collapse that followed the Revolution, states passed debt-relief laws and printed paper money with abandon. The measures won favor from suffering constituents, but they created a chaotic business climate and threatened, in the words of Alexander Hamilton, to *relax the springs of industry.*

In 1787, fifty-five of the nation's political elites met in Philadelphia to address the alarming threats to property. They were followers of the Puritan philosopher John Locke, who believed that of the trinity of natural rights—life, liberty, property—it was property that government could best protect. Secure the rights of ownership and the other rights would follow. Locke called property *the fence* to freedom.

In England, promoters of enclosure argued against planting as fences hedges like medlar, which produce an edible fruit. The fence itself might provide the commoners with a means of sustenance.

Quince

Honeysuckle

Pear

Chokecherry

Dogwood

Bridal-wreath Spirea

not flowers but bone, worn by stress and use

Summer brings a spate of tree felling to the cemetery. Rumor has it that the new superintendent plans to return the overgrown sections to a more manicured, Victorian look. One day, at the place the birders call the four corners, I find the massive white oak cut down, its leaves and branches scattered across the ground. The trunk has been split into sections and heaped around the ragged stump. It is large enough to lie across, so I do, face down, smelling gasoline and hot sawdust. I count a hundred rings before a green pulls up and tells me to move back outside the caution tape.

* * *

Homer Simpson BEST DAD IN THE HOUSE balloon
ATLANTIC CITY magnet with tiny jackpot slots
porcelain turtle with flowers sprouting out of its back
pebbles with orange and yellow elf hats glued on
NERDY BIRD™ with wings on springs
HEAR NO EVIL, SEE NO EVIL, frogs with a fourth covering its crotch

* * *

April 9, 2003. U.S. troops cross the Tigris into Freedom Square, central Baghdad. Residents bang at a forty-foot statue of Saddam Hussein with sledge hammers before U.S. Marines loop a chain around its neck and pull it down with a tank. The next day, New York Governor George Pataki addresses a rally of construction workers at the World Trade Center. He calls for Hussein's statue to be melted down and added to the rebuilt site.

A few months later, in Amite City, Louisiana, workers clad in silver heat-resistant suits pour twenty-four tons of molten steel into a mold before flashing cameras. The metal—from the south tower of the World Trade Center—will form the bow stem of the Navy ship USS New York. *This piece of steel has been washed with the tears of Americans and hardened by millions of prayers from around the world*, proclaims the president of Northrop Grumman Ship Systems.

The balance of steel from the towers, 285,000 tons, went to scrap dealers in New Jersey, says architecture writer Philip Nobel. It likely returned to U.S. shores as *toasters* and *Toyotas*.

so the weapon wears its wound

In January 1787, tensions over property in the new nation came to a boil. A few thousand farmers led by Continental Army captain Daniel Shays marched through four feet of snow to capture the government arsenal at Springfield, Massachusetts. The enraged farmers, many of them veterans of the Revolution, felt betrayed by independence. To rid itself of war debts, the state levied stiff taxes, then confiscated the land of those unable to pay.

The farmers wanted only to keep their fields, but the rumor quickly spread that they were dangerous radicals out to redistribute all property. The specter of this *leveling spirit*—an echo of the widespread revolts in England against the Enclosure Acts—drove men like George Washington and James Madison to the Philadelphia convention. They wanted to bolster the federal government against such populist threats. Says the legal scholar Jennifer Nedelsky: *Fear is a basic element* in the framework of the U.S. Constitution.

In England, the enclosers argued that allowing commoners to remain on the land was like leaving America to the "savages": *Let the poor native Indians . . . enjoy all their ancient privileges, and cultivate their country their own way.* The idea could not be allowed to take root. Common lands must *submit to the yoke of improvement.*

a wing wider than war

* * *

Real estate developer Larry Silverstein felt fated to rebuild the World Trade Center. Though he signed the lease on the twin towers just weeks before the planes hit, he had long coveted the buildings. He felt his own Seven World Trade *looked like a peanut* beside them. Silverstein's parents emigrated from Eastern Europe to one of Brooklyn's poorest neighborhoods. He convinced his father to go into business and gradually built himself a real estate empire.

The legal scholar Jennifer Nedelsky's father also emigrated to America. Leo Nedelsky fought with the White Army during the Bolshevik revolution and ended up escaping into China. He came to America and studied theoretical physics as one of Robert Oppenheimer's first students. When Oppenheimer went to Los Alamos to build the atomic bombs, Leo declined to join him.

Nedelsky says that the framers of the Constitution sought to protect not just property, but unequal property. Riches sprang from *the unequal faculties for acquiring them*, wrote Madison. He considered it *the first object of government* to protect these God-given abilities, and their fruits, as an aspect of individual liberty.

to impregnate the waters of the world

The ancient shoreline of Manhattan island runs through the middle of the World Trade Center. The architect Daniel Libeskind designed the Freedom Tower to stand on land reclaimed from the muddy flow of the Hudson River. Silverstein tried to convince public officials to reduce engineering costs by moving the tower. He chafed against the *government interference* at the site. He bought an oil painting depicting a ship on a rough sea as a metaphor for himself. *This ship is going to make it.*

The word "estate" as landed property appeared in American English, 1623. The same year the first sawmill in the colonies, near York, Maine, started cutting timber.

The British Royal Navy consumed whole forests for its ships. Main masts required trunks as wide as 40 inches and as tall as 120 feet. Few trees this large remained in Europe, so British authorities claimed for the crown the giant white pines of upper New England. Agents of His Majesty's Navy raised the ire of landowners by marching through Maine and New Hampshire marking the largest trees with the royal arrow.

cross all words with fire

* * *

Cleaveland means cliffs, an edge place, by way of "ail" and "ear." In 1796, the year Nehemiah *first drew vital breath,* his uncle Moses founded a settlement at the mouth of the Cuyahoga River after sailing, lost, along the Erie shore.

Moses bribed a delegation of Mohawks and Senecas to relinquish their claims to the lands of the Western Reserve. They didn't have much choice: The Revolutionary War general represented a group of Connecticut land speculators. They had just purchased the entire three million acres.

DO NOT ENTER ANY PLOT OF STRANGER

The Brooke Russell Astor Reading Room for Rare Books and Manuscripts requires I.D. and a special form. Occupation: writer. Purpose: poetry. I expect at any moment for someone to call my bluff, the shape of ships

bearing strange landscapes
from America. *Here mark the edges*
of an ancient shore we climb
the names for, echoing

an ache   a wet
           thread back

The Founders denounced those who got rich off speculating in paper money; they viewed it as an *Inlet to Luxury & Folly.* Getting rich off the land, on the other hand, was perfectly in keeping with the values of the republic. Here was wealth that could be touched and smelled and tasted: It implied hard work and civilization. Washington himself amassed more than 500,000 acres, some of it purchased illegally from natives.

Bluff in the sense "deception" comes from the *criminal underground* that spread through London as enclosures and other social changes displaced the rural population. *London emerged as the urban equivalent of the greenwood forest,* says the historian John McMullen. The upper classes developed an obsession with this culture and its secret cant language. Dozens of criminal biographies appeared, and glossaries promised to decode *the tongues of rogues.*

* * *

polar bear reading *101 Snow Games* to a penguin baby
miniature I LOVE YOU orange traffic cone
Inca Kola® bottle filled with holy water
porcelain turkey in graduation robes
'69crs BROOKLYN MOTORCYCLE CLUB sticker
DEAR PAPA WE WISH WE GOT THE CHANCE TO MEET YOU card

* * *

New York Governor DeWitt Clinton came up with the idea of linking Lake Erie to the Hudson River through a 363-mile canal—a water highway that would bring New York products to the interior of the country and make the city the world's financial capital. David Bates Douglass supervised part of the massive project.

Clinton was the first to sail on the Erie Canal in 1825, in a packet boat called the Seneca Chief. When he reached New York, he emptied two casks from Lake Erie into the Atlantic in a ceremonial "Wedding of the Waters."

Cleaveland describes the depiction on the bronze monument at Clinton's grave in Green-Wood:

> The bustling scene around the boats and the dock is happily contrasted with the idle group of Indians, who seem to be looking in sadness on the enterprise, before which they and their bark canoes are fading fast away.

In *The Earth Shall Weep*, James Wilson notes the tendency among white writers to imbue the natives with an aura of ghostliness, as if they disappeared not from systematic extermination but of their own mysterious accord.

Red cedar
Mountain laurel
Swiss stone pine
Honey locust
Weeping cherry
Spanish bayonet

When Cleaveland's uncle Moses reached the Cuyahoga River, he beheld *a beautiful plain covered with luxuriant forest-growth*. He determined the spot would be ideal for a city. The mapmaker who surveyed lots for sale spelled Cleaveland without its "a." *The low-back-wide vowel, formed with the widest opening of jaws, pharynx, and lips.*

In one hundred years, most of the *vast ocean of dark green forest* that covered the state of Ohio—nearly twenty-four million acres—would be gone. A century after that, the Cuyahoga River, choked with pollution, would catch on fire.

* * *

The black granite tombstone of STEVEN CHARLES VINCENT has a map of Iraq engraved with AL-BASRAH marked. DEC. 31, 1955 – AUG. 2, 2005 AND FLIGHTS OF ANGELS SING THEE TO THY REST. BELOVED WIFE LISA RAMACI AUG. 4, 1956 – awaits her end date.

In dirt at the base of the stone lie a bottle of Bombay Sapphire, a package of cigars in faded wrapping paper, two miniature U.S. flags on sticks, and a red LOVE YOU teddy bear in a plastic bag.

Vincent was the first U.S. journalist killed in the war. Two days after he published a piece in the *New York Times* about corruption in the Basra police force, gunmen shot and killed him. They also shot his Iraqi interpreter, Nooriya Taiz. She survived.

One morning I pass three people at Vincent's grave site. A woman with long black hair, jean jacket tied around her waist, takes pictures of an old man and woman, each leaning on a cane beside the shining stone. *Of course* I hear the younger woman say, irritation in her voice. Then all three stand in silence, looking down at the dirt.

A few months after Vincent died, the *Times* reported that he and Taiz had fallen in love and planned to marry. Lisa Ramaci told the paper they were only getting married so Taiz could get out of Iraq. "I may sound like the self-deluded, cuckolded wife," she said, "but believe me, as sure as God made Cleveland, he would've come home to me."

* * *

Andrew Jackson Downing, muse of Emerson's orchard, designed the grounds of the White House, the Smithsonian, and the U.S. Capitol. He also proposed the idea for Central Park before he died in a steam ship explosion at age thirty-six.

In his massive *Treatise on the Theory and Practice of Landscape Gardening*, Downing lays out his vision of the nation as a vast Eden sculpted by individual property owners. He devotes most of the *Treatise* to trees. In addition to *ministering to our daily wants*, he proclaims them among *the most beautiful objects in nature*. Downing categorizes trees according to their *expression*: round-headed, pyramidal, and spiry-topped. Round-headed trees—oak, ash, beech, walnut—make essential composition objects because *they reflect differently the lights and produce deep shadows*.

In 2006, the *New York Times* praised the World Trade Center memorial design as *stunningly simple . . . a forest grove around two large voids* marking where the towers once stood. In fact, the original design consisted of an austere, empty plaza. But the judges who selected the memorial worried it would be too stark for a public remembrance. They asked for trees to *serve as symbols of renewal*.

In designing Green-Wood, Douglass followed Downing's principles. He sought to preserve the *variety of surface* and the *picturesque scenery* of the place. But perfecting these features required, as Cleaveland noted, *the constant use of the rake and roller, the scythe, and the weeding-hook.*

> Those who have not watched the long and skillful and patient operation—the scooping and the rounding—the taking out and the filling in—the digging down and the heaping up—can hardly imagine how much has been done in the way of shaping and improving the contour of these grounds.

The forest that frightened the Pilgrims also was shaped by human labor. The earliest documents complain not about the trees but about the distance the settlers had to go to find fuel wood: *half a quarter of an English mile*. Over the centuries, Native Americans burned the trees to open up fields and planted fruit and nut-bearing species—acorn, beech, chestnut. According to the historian Charles Mann, in colonial times as many as one quarter of the trees in the East were native American chestnuts.

By the time the Mayflower touched the shores of Cape Cod, this ecological order was collapsing. So many natives had been wiped out by disease that they could no longer maintain the land. The forest soon covered maize fields and garden plots. Where the Pilgrims saw a *desolate willdernes*, they actually were looking at graves.

* * *

plastic baby doll wearing a cop uniform
sleeping cherub cuddling a bunny
MATCHBOX® ambulance with windshield crack
Las Vegas Betty Boop magnet
Camel cigarette label carved in granite
smiling ghosts arm in arm

* * *

Today my first encounter with a wood duck in winter plumage. An improbably beautiful bird, it has a delicate dark head and red eyes outlined in white. I stand watching and sketching it for a long time. I want to think I have found something rare, but it is common. What I find here are the scavengers and adapters, what survives in the margins—in sewage ponds and suburban lakes, on high rises and utility poles—heron, egret, wood duck, raccoon, squirrel, and hawk.

* * *

Mockernut

Mountain-Ash

Rose-of-Sharon

False-Cypress

Hazel

Azalea

Downing lamented that America lacked the large estates necessary to recreate the *splendid landscape gardens* of England. But he felt optimistic that the nation's many small landowners could be taught to beautify the country by avoiding a *ridiculous* emulation of the rich and *embellishing in accordance with propriety.* Improving the land also would help the restless settler *grow a strong attachment to the natal soil . . . strengthening his patriotism, and making him a better citizen.*

a skin to war in

The Dawes Act of 1887 aimed to *emancipate* American Indians by transforming them into property-owning Americans. The law divided reservation land into tracts of 160 acres and authorized the government to sell off any unclaimed lots. As long as they owned land in common, declared Senator Dawes, indigenous people would remain savage, lacking the *selfishness* that lies *at the bottom of civilization.*

Cherokee Chief Dennis Bushyhead responded to the Senator:

> [Land], like the air and waters, is the heritage of the people; if it were otherwise, our domain would soon drift into the hands of a few, and our poor people, in a few years, would become like your poor people, most of whom, if they died to-morrow, do not own a foot of the earth's surface in which they could be buried.

In 1853, after the death of his twin infant sons, Henry Ward Beecher purchased a retreat from his Brooklyn parish—ninety-six-acre Blossom Farm in the Berkshires. On his land stood a massive American elm he named "the Queen." *When I whispered to myself, This is mine, there was a shrinking as if there were sacrilege in the very thought of property in such a creature of God.*

The Germanic word for god had no gender. It shifted to masculine after the coming of the Christian religion. In *The Dream of the Rood*, one of the earliest Anglo-Saxon Christian poems, the tree on which Jesus was crucified speaks. It describes becoming one in suffering with *the Savior*, pierced with the same *dark nails* and *sodden* with his blood.

* * *

DUBBLE BUBBLE™ toy basketball
Mylar balloon sun with sunglasses on
teddy bear wearing an American flag suit
porcelain cat with a rosary around its neck
postcard from DR. ELLEN D. PAN, M.D.: *Wishing*
you a healthy dose
of birthday
cheer this year!

* * *

My ancestors, the "Cobbs," pollarded the trees of the English forests, whacking them back to the trunk so they would sprout quick-growing wood for timber and fuel.

According to the arborist William Bryant Logan, in people and place names everywhere exist traces of ancient forests. Not only Woods, but also Bradley, Brando, Chase, and Teller derive from trees. The children of uncertain parentage born of Midsummer's Eve revelries in the woods were called Johnson, for St. John's Day, Robinson, son of Robin Hood, or Everson, son of Eve.

For its memorial grove, the World Trade Center Foundation selected more than three hundred trees from New York, Pennsylvania, and D.C. According to the Foundation's four-page press release, the trees are being "held" at a nursery in nearby New Jersey, so that they can grow accustomed to *a climate that resembles the World Trade Center.* They are pruned, fertilized, watered, and protected from pests. Those that can't adjust—the weak and the dying—will be "culled" before planting.

The architects chose sweet gum and swamp white oak trees for the memorial because they are hardy and durable. The two species also resemble one another, *allowing for a uniform feel* at the site. However, the Foundation assures, *the trees will never be identical, neither to each other nor from year to year, a clear reminder that they are living individuals.*

In 1881, Vincent van Gogh wrote his brother Theo that in order to paint a landscape, he had to first capture the essence of the trees: *If one draws a pollard willow as if it were a living being . . . the surroundings follow almost by themselves.*

Less than a decade later, van Gogh would be dead, having shot himself in the heart.

In 1832, still grieving the death of his wife, and nearly sick to death himself, Emerson traveled to Europe. He returned home the following year with new energy and purpose, inspired by the famed Cabinet of Natural History in Paris to write his book *Nature.* But the old despair still lingered. As the weeks-long journey over the ocean began, he mused on the ever-present possibility of shipwreck and wrote in his journal: *I am glad to be on my way home, yet not so glad as others, and my way to the bottom I could find perchance with less regret, for I think it would not hurt me.*

Regret comes from the Old French word for lament.

* * *

In 2002, New York City Mayor Michael Bloomberg attempted to contact all the families of firefighters who died at the World Trade Center. He recalled his experience to the judges selecting the memorial. Most people were moving on, he said, but *there were fifteen-odd families, where the spouse, I think it was probably all women, they just kept crying and crying. It's not my business to say that to a woman, 'Suck it up and get going,' but that is the way I feel. You've got to look to the future.*

The words "suck," "cry," and "sigh" are all onomatopoetic. Cry comes from the Latin word for pig squeal.

In his writings, Cleaveland provides almost no information about his life. One autobiographical summary lists his children: *Joseph M., a graduate of Princeton, now Superintendent of the State Hospital for the Insane at Poughkeepsie, N.Y.; George N., a graduate of Yale, now a farmer in Westport, Conn.; Henry W., an architect in San Francisco; Abby E.*

My wife died in 1836, he reports. *In 1842 I married Katherine Atherton . . . she died in 1846.*

Cleaveland published his first book on the cemetery the year of his second wife's death. But she is not buried there, and he mentions her nowhere else. Perhaps he followed his own advice: *Confine your passionate utterances to the friendly bosoms that share your grief; or, still better, breathe them only in your secret sighs.*

In "Social Aims," Emerson professes admiration for republican restraint: *Self-control is the rule. You have in you there a noisy, sensual savage which you are to keep down.* But Emerson's own grief was unseemly. A year after his first wife died, Emerson dug her up so he could see her. A quarter century later, he dug up his beloved five-year-old son Waldo. Of these experiences, Emerson recorded nothing.

In the days after September 11, Rudy Giuliani urged New Yorkers to return to life as usual. *Go to restaurants*, he said. *Go shopping. Show that you're not afraid.*

the eye is the first circle

Show that you're not afraid.

* * *

teddy bear wearing a mets uniform

TROLLZ® doll with neon green hair and glitter comb

Spiderman web-slinging action figure

turtle holding a rainbow umbrella

weathered greeting card with a sad elephant in purple hat

sitting beneath a single star: *How I wonder how you are*

MISS YOU *Dear Brother John*

Love You, Sis Joan.

Two balloon heads on strings have been drawn in ballpoint

and labeled "you" and "me" *ha! ha!*

* * *

Mount Auburn Cemetery in Boston got its name from an English village destroyed by enclosure. Trespassing Harvard students named the tract of wooded land after Oliver Goldsmith's lament for the village:

> . . . scourged by famine from the smiling land,
> The mournful peasant leads his humble band;
> And while he sinks, without one arm to save,
> The country blooms—a garden, and a grave.

In his book *1491,* Charles Mann claims that the ideals of liberty and equality pervading the colonies came partly from the Native Americans who surrounded them. Many indigenous societies north of the Rio Grande had a *formidable tradition of limited government and personal autonomy.* Mann says that the image of *Indian freedom,* which first appeared at the Boston tea party, has recurred through the centuries, most recently when protestors in China, South Korea, and Ukraine dressed as Native Americans.

Nedelsky says property in America has maintained the quality of myth. Its status is that of an inviolable natural right, not a social construct that requires government to define and enforce. The result: Property has been removed completely from the realm of democratic debate.

Fall 2006. Workers find arm bones and leg bones, wallets, shoes, and watches in a sewer opening one block away from the World Trade Center. The hole was covered by a road paved in 2002 to speed rebuilding, despite warnings from recovery workers that more remains might be found there.

Soon after trucks began rumbling over the road, the state unveiled its first proposals for the site. The plans met with a wave of public criticism for cramming ten million feet of commercial space onto a square mile of earth now *saturated with flesh.*

The owner and leaseholder have certain rights, explained one official. *These plans all represent respecting these private property rights . . .*

The romantic garden was supposed to provide uninterrupted, unfenced views of the surrounding country. But wandering herds had to be kept out, so gardeners invented the "ha-ha," a sunken, brick-lined trench that acted as an invisible fence.

* * *

63

Cleaveland's grave is easy to find. He lies beneath the only tree in the lot, a vast purple beech with scarred and gnarled trunk. About twelve feet up it splits into five limbs the size of trees themselves. A thin metal wire protrudes from either side of the split. BILLY TOGA carved his name twice in the ugly trunk; the date 1957 has been painted on with what looks like tar. One section of the tree has died, its bare branches reaching like a claw up to the sky.

The grave is marked by a tapering, seven-foot granite slab, unadorned except for a standard vine scroll carved across the top.

Nothing acknowledges Cleaveland's role as the chronicler of Green-Wood. He was living with his son George when he died, and George, who died a few months later, lies beneath the same marker. Probably the two caskets are stacked.

> I WILL RANSOM THEM FROM THE
> POWER OF THE GRAVE; I WILL
> REDEEM THEM FROM DEATH.

Next door, beneath a smaller granite marker lies Cleaveland's daughter. ABBY ELIZABETH CLEAVELAND, 1832-1907. IN ZEAL A MARTHA WITH A MARY'S HEART.

Granite comes from the melting heat of the earth. Much of it is at least 500 million years old, from before animals or plants existed. It was not Cleaveland's favorite stone. *It has a stern, cold look,* he wrote.

The Old Testament Nehemiah rebuilt the walls of Jerusalem, *one hand laboring and the other holding his weapon.*

Mary, of unknown origin, said to mean, literally, "rebellion."

For want of beauty, I place my face against the granite. In its reflection I see my own eye, the graves behind me, sky and trees. I reach out my tongue to touch the stone.

The gesture makes me a stranger. *Blank*

a gleaming creature.

* * *

III. THE FOREIGN BIRDS

GHOST: The sense of the pre-Teutonic *ghoizdo-z* should be "fury, anger". . . the root *gheis* appears with cognate sense in Old Norse *geisa* to rage, Gothic *usgaisjan* to terrify (see gast v.); outside Teutonic the derivatives seem to point to a primary sense "to wound, tear, pull to pieces."

Black smoke billows from the crematorium beside the gate. Heat pouring out makes the sky and trees wavy. The smell—hot drill on bone in the dentist's chair, and something else, an acrid, charred whiff. It mixes with the yeasty drift of bread from the bakery down the street and the noxious smell of the MY FAVORITE PLASTIC factory.

> *the vanished*
> *dress us in skin*

The Internet Cremation Society explains that it takes between two and three hours to vaporize organs and other soft tissue, leaving four to six pounds of bone that is ground up into "cremains," a portmanteau to disguise raw meaning.

Monk parrots screech past as I walk up the tree-lined path. Legend has it they escaped from a shipment at Kennedy airport in the 1960s. They hang like green jewels from bristling stick nests high in the Gothic gate. Green-Wood tolerates their messy habits and constant chatter because they drive away pigeons, most loathed among birds, whose acidic droppings eat through the old stone.

The government tried to wipe out monk parrots in New York, but eventually gave up. Other states gas or shoot them because they nest on warm transmission lines and transformers. In their native Argentina, where they are considered crop pests, hundreds of thousands have been killed or shipped to the United States for pets. Poachers in Brooklyn sometimes capture entire feral colonies. The birds bring high prices in pet stores because they are good talkers and can develop large vocabularies.

"Speak" echoes

        the Latin verb "to scatter." A metaphor. Say words
        came from a whole before   a tree

  or flying thing

> *Now I take off my uni-*
> *form and come back*
> *to life pregnant all*
> *waters the world*
>
>   *(ghostword)*

* * *

The first warm spring day orange warning signs line the walks: PESTICIDE
SPRAYING KEEP OUT FOR 24 HOURS. The familiar chemical smell seeps
into my nostrils. I change directions, but every turn reveals another guy
with hose spewing yellow poison. I'm moving fast now, shirt over mouth,
breathing hard, sucking in the stuff despite myself. "You shouldn't be here
when we're spraying," one calls out, kind of nice. "What about you," I say
back. He shrugs, the movie of himself. "It's a paycheck." So, another death
(the word for it). But I'm turning away already.

During the period of his cemetery obsession, Cleaveland produced his only
literary text, a translation of *Les Fleurs Animées*. The book is part parody of
popular ladies' botanies, part sincere guide to horticulture. It relates the
tales of flowers who rebelled against the goddess Flora and walked the earth
in female form.

the in, in, in

I climb to the top of Battle Hill where the sprayers haven't reached yet. I sit
at the base of Minerva and watch two workers knock bricks out of the old
vegetable warehouse across the street. Wind comes up, still with a winter
bite. The sound of metal on clay rings through the clear air. One of them
sees me, and waves. Caught, I wipe the saltwater off my face. This morning I
received the verdict for month number twelve: not pregnant.

Tongue the awkward *l* into *v*, root of Old English "to leave."

Now the doctors can agree something "real"
might be wrong inside me *(that which twists the lips)*.

In Roman mythology, the West Wind raped the earth-nymph Chloris, and
she transformed into Flora, goddess of flowers. As she spoke roses fell out of
her mouth.

The word "pregnant" was taboo in written English until the sixteenth
century. Euphemisms include "poisoned" *(in reference to the swelling)*.

* * *

In 2006, Green-Wood sprayed herbicides throughout its five hundred acres fall and spring to keep weeds from sprouting. The year before, New York City banned from public property two of the chemicals used in Green-Wood—pendimethalin and 2,4-D. Pendimethalin poisons fish and frogs. 2,4-D was a major component of Agent Orange, which the United States used to destroy the crops and jungles of Vietnam.

According to Cornell University, rats fed 2,4-D gave birth to babies with wavy ribs, *a function of general toxicity*.

poison arrow (a bird)

flight ignites

to impregnate all waters   the world

Ladies' botanies became best sellers during the nineteenth century, thanks to advances in the science of plants and the popularity of gardening among the middle class. Botany was seen as an appropriate pursuit for a young woman, who *feels all that delight in [flowers] which seems so naturally to belong to her age and sex.*

(a form of being lost)

One scholar calls ladies' botanies *transgenred.* They combined science with poetry, quotations from scripture, and flower fables, in which plants personified as women deliver moral lessons. According to the historian Vera Norwood, this was a way of disguising the science so that it would appeal to female readers. But it also kept women among the ranks of the amateurs. Such heteroglossic books were not serious.

The New York State pesticide registry contains more than thirteen thousand products. Their names march in order:

Barren
Battleship
Bicep
Black Flag
Blast Off
Blitz
Breathe Easy

* * *

Les Fleurs Animées contains fifty-two hand-colored engravings of women-flowers by the French caricaturist J.J. Grandville. This makes it valuable: It sells online for more than $1,000.

The New York Public Library owns four editions of the book in its George Arents Collection on Tobacco. Arents, from Virginia, grew rich off the business and became obsessed. He collected thousands of items of "tobacciana."

His collection includes the original handwritten manuscript of *The Importance of Being Earnest* because the plot involves a cigarette case. *The Flowers Personified* is there because it contains a fable about the tobacco plant. Arents himself never smoked.

In the low-lit, wood-paneled room, I present my I.D. and ask to view this book. A librarian is summoned and disappears again. I have read that the collection is contained in a Georgian-style sitting room donated by Arents, but I am not invited into this sanctum. The librarian comes back with the object cradled on green foam wedges. She sets it in front of me and, smiling, hands me a weighted rope—"the snake"—to hold the pages open.

At first I am afraid to touch the brittle book. I sit looking at the blue cloth cover embossed with gold flowers. The less friendly librarian, a man, taps the green-shaded lamp above me in case I want to turn it on. I don't turn it on. I do. I read *823 .mR stpircsunaM dna skooB eraR rof mooR gnidaeR rotsA llessuR ekoorB ehT* on the glass transom. From a newspaper folded on the table beside me shines the face of the brain-erased woman in Florida whom George W. Bush will this night order back to life.

> *Lit a live*
> *look* I think
> fire that through
> the blind
> stem drives
> the breath grief
> a kind
> of self a skin
> to war in

* * *

Brute
Butcher's Bath
Butcher's Blue Skies
Camelot
Can't Bite Me

The study of botany could be dangerous for ladies. Linnaeus created a system for classifying plants based on sex organs, which he referred to in Greek as the "husband" *(andria)* and "wife" *(gynia)*. Most flowers, however, aren't monogamous. This aspect of the science had to be kept from young women, or sexual anarchy could result. The 1798 poem "Unsex'd Females" expresses this anxiety:

> For puberty in sighing florets pant,
> Or point the prostitution of a plant;
> Dissect its organ of unhallow'd lust,
> And fondly gaze the titillating dust.

Opening any field of science to women threatened the social order. The *Ladies' Botany* section of *Les Fleurs Animées* makes the danger explicit with a warning: *Stop here, fair readers. Go no farther. Put down the book . . . they wish to make you scientific.*

The author of the *Ladies' Botany* skirts the Linnaean controversy: *We shall avoid here the use of those scientific terms, which . . . have no other effect than to distort pretty mouths into ugly grimaces.*

To "ping" (short for Packet Internet Groper) means to send a signal out over cyberspace seeking an answer to ensure messages are getting through. It also is called *echo request.*

In a hysterosalpingogram, a doctor sends liquid dye through the fallopian tubes during an x-ray to get a picture of their shape. *The pain may be acute, depending on the force with which the doctor injects the liquid.*

> hysteria: *not simply "womb"*
> *but rather the womb as an animal*
> *on the move within the body*

That humiliating cry. It did not come from me.

* * *

In ancient Greece, mourners hired professional women to voice their grief. They transformed speech into wailing, giving vent to the pain of the bereaved and even speaking directly to the dead, an ability only they had. But this power also posed dangers, it could fuel violent emotions and even spark bloody revenge.

> *What you touched*
> *with your dark*
> *mouths, we*
> *on our bellies*
> *thirst for it*

"Clomid," says the doctor, handing me a prescription. It forces the body to produce more than one egg each month, raising the risk of multiple fetuses. I want to know how many. "We can make you release as many eggs at once as we want, as many as twenty," he tells me. "Of course, we would never do that."

As goddess of fertility, Flora caused the birth of Mars, *who leads the army in battle*. Ovid has her confess this in the *Fasti*, his epic poem on the Roman pantheon. Juno grieved that Jupiter had not coupled with her to produce Minerva, who sprang from his forehead. She went to complain to Oceanus about her plight and, tired from her journey, stopped at Flora's door. When Flora tries to console her, Juno replies:

> My grief is not to be assuaged with words. If Jupiter has
> become a father without the use of a wife . . . why should I
> despair of becoming a mother without a husband . . .? I will try
> all the drugs in the wide world.

Solon banned public lament in Athens in the sixth century BCE. Women could mourn only inside private houses, and only blood relatives could accompany the corpse to the grave before dawn. The poet Tina Darragh says that privatizing grief in this way hid the consequences of war from the rest of society. Grief became a "family" matter only.

Official Greek art forms co-opted the power of lament. The encomium transformed rage into public praise for those killed in battle. Greek tragedies depict lament as a dark force threatening the city.

My heart would have outrun speech to break forth the water of its grief (Agamemnon).

* * *

Dog tags glint from dirt beside the grave of SGT. MICHAEL RIVERA JUNE 6, 1984-MARCH 7, 2007. PRESIDENTIAL PRAYER TEAM ONE NATION UNDER GOD is printed on one of the tags above an American flag. KILLZONE™ LIBERATION reads the other. A cartoon soldier with glowing eyes stares down the barrel of a gun.

"Gun" comes from the Old Norse female name Gunilda. The OED notes the common link between powerful weapons and women. See also Big Bertha, Black Maria, Coughing Clara, the Dolly Parton tank, and Gilda the atomic bomb.

Sergeant Rivera's dark-eyed daughter grins and reaches for the camera in the YouTube tribute to him made by his cousin. She turned six months old the day before a bomb exploded in Baghdad and killed him.

In his laser-engraved tombstone portrait, Sergeant Rivera wears a dress uniform and service beret. He has a slight smirk and one eyebrow subtly arched.

I pull a folded piece of paper from a bouquet of half-dead flowers. Neat cursive covers both sides. Someone has written his name over and over.

What wound
spills forth from
its own shining
mouth to give
birth to the dark
    earth: flood marks

* * *

Daybreak
Deadsure
Dead-Fast
Dead eye
Deadline
Deep Woods

On Clomid I produce ten eggs at once and a large cyst, so the doctor won't inseminate. He tells me to come back in a few months.

I go down the hole opened by flowers. Grandville fought on the barricades during the French revolution of 1830. Afterward, when Louis Philippe took the throne, Grandville joined the attack against the monarchy and became the most popular political cartoonist in France.

Since a large part of the population couldn't read, the censors feared images more than they feared words. They repeatedly fined the papers, forcing the artists to invent new symbols for dissent. To represent the obese King, they began using a pear, French slang for "fat-head." Soon images of pears appeared everywhere across Paris. The art historian Judith Wechsler calls the strategy a *submersion of words into silence.*

Plato banned poetry from his ideal city because it might arouse dangerous emotions. He points to Homer's depiction in the *Iliad* of Achilles passionately lamenting the slaying of his friend Patroklos in the Trojan War. Like a woman, such imagery might seduce men into unleashing their own feelings; they might lose control over *the city within.*

who grows ashamed before the blown rose

Those who longed to see inside the human body had to settle for animals until the sixteenth century, when anatomy suddenly flowered. Taboos against dissection fell away and the corpses of criminals and poor people filled the medical theatres. Anatomists performed before a paying audience.

Andreas Vesalius pioneered this practice. His main work, *On the Fabric of the Human Body,* features a crowd pressed around the cut open corpse of a woman. He reports that *in fear of being hanged [she] declared herself pregnant.* When the authorities discovered her lie, they hanged her, and gave her body to the doctor. Vesalius doesn't name her original crime.

* * *

Summer 2008, the seventh year of the war, monsters begin to appear. A doglike animal with a toothed beak washes up on Montauk. A sheriff's deputy in Texas videotapes a chupacabra along the Mexico border. Three hunters in Georgia capture Bigfoot, and a two-headed turtle appears, and then disappears from a Brooklyn pet shop.

When he arrived in Paris, the grieving Emerson fell in love—not with a person but with a museum. The renowned Cabinet of Natural History collected plants and animals from around the globe and displayed them *bone to bone, lung to lung, and brain to brain.*

The Ornithological Chambers most enchanted Emerson. The variety of stuffed birds from all corners of the world filled him with a sense of limitless life and possibility. Among the species Emerson most admired were the birds of paradise from New Guinea, with their flowing plumes and iridescent colors. The man whose wife had died two years earlier wrote that the collection made him feel *calm and genial as a bridegroom.*

the face destroyed in the free soil

The Cabinet also inspired Grandville. He found in its exotic species an *infinite reserve* of ideas for his animal-human caricatures. Grandville visited the museum with his friend Daumier, who had just spent six months in jail for his drawings. The police also harassed Grandville, and the thought of being taken filled him with terror. After seeing Daumier he wrote in his journal: *thoughts from earlier on grab hold of me again: chagrin—fear . . . Pain again—at the lithographic presses disgust for what I am doing—fears.*

The Kaluli people of Papua New Guinea believe the dead often turn into flying things. The birds of paradise that delighted Emerson to the Kaluli embody the spirits of women—although they are biologically male, their cascading plumage recalls ladies in colorful skirts seductively swinging their hips.

The word "fallopian" comes from the student of Vesalius who first examined the organs inside the body of an anonymous cadaver. He named the vagina, *asserted the existence of the hymen in virgins*, and described the clitoris, as well as the workings of the inner ear. He never determined the tubes' purpose. He called them the *trumpets* of the uterus.

After Emerson opened his wife's grave, she began to fade from his journals.

* * *

Earth-Tone
Echo
Eclipse
Eliminator
Embark

The Cabinet of Natural History overflowed with new life forms gathered from distant worlds—the spoils of colonial exploits. It exuded commerce and empire. It also implied death. As the Emerson scholar Brown points out: *The organism itself (unless it was fortunate enough to be selected for the menagerie. . .) had to be dissected, preserved, and encased.*

Among the items in the catalog when Emerson visited:

2,625 entire skeletons
2,150 skulls
1,867 sets of viscera
1,437 sense organs
479 genital organs
878 fetuses
197 "monsters"

The French censors outlawed all images of pears. The newspapers rebelled, publishing the injunction in the shape of a pear and harassing the officials with drawings that echoed pear shapes. Finally, in 1835 the monarchy declared total censorship and shut down the political papers. Wechsler says that censorship pushed Grandville from *speaking silence into silent silence.* He turned to making strange, visionary books.

The fathers of the Christian Church adopted Plato's ban on lament. Greeks considered public grieving dangerous, as if it were contagious. To the Christians, even private grief smacked of blasphemy—a sign of doubt about God's power to bestow eternal life.

> *looking back for anything*
> *not burning*

In February 2009, President Barack Obama eased the twenty-year ban on images of soldiers' bodies returning from war (*hard light, clear edges*). Now each family gets to decide whether to allow public witnesses.

* * *

I'm watching through binoculars as the egret hunts in Valley Water. It moves slowly, almost imperceptibly, tilting toward the thick mat of lilies. In a flash, it lunges and comes up with something speared on its beak. It shakes its head, trying to work the thing off. I watch for what seems a long time as it shakes and tilts, prey still impaled. Finally, it gives a prodigious jerk and the creature falls at its feet. The egret lifts its head, looks around, and takes off, spooked by something—maybe me. I watch it flap with slow, awkward beats over the trees.

I walk over to look. A fat tadpole the length of my palm lies on the shore. It is part frog—legs have sprouted from either side of its tail. The egret pierced it right through the middle, guts spilling out of the hole. The one eye turned skyward shifts, registering my shadow. Its tadpole gills move methodically, drawing in useless air. I leave it there, hoping the egret will come back for its meal.

* * *

In 1852 Green-Wood conducted its own natural history experiment. To add Old World charm to the grounds, it imported 168 birds from England. Cleaveland lists the inventory from the bill of sale:

48 skylarks
24 woodlarks
48 goldfinches
24 robins
12 thrushes
12 blackbirds

Of these, he reports, *the woodlarks were the most costly, the thrushes and blackbirds coming next, and the average price being a fraction over eightpence a bird.*

The Kaluli believe that women who mourn the dead turn into birds. Their lament cries echo calls from the surrounding forest, expressing loss *beyond the resources of talk.*

> *a dry sea, fragile*
> from "to cut with a sharp point"

Kaluli laments use *impregnated language* says Steven Feld, the musician and anthropologist who wrote the definitive study on Kaluli poetics. The words carry metaphoric meaning: A list of place names associated with a person who has died brings forth the events of that person's life and achieves the goal of the singing—to make the audience weep.

St. Augustine on the death of his mother: *I closed her eyes; and there flowed in a great sadness on my heart and it was passing into tears, when at the strong behest of my mind my eyes sucked back the fountain dry, and sorrow was in me like a convulsion.*

In Grandville's *Private and Public Lives of Animals,* the inhabitants of the Natural History Cabinet rise up against their human masters.

Next to a margin note that reads "A FAILURE." Cleaveland reports that all the birds disappeared.

* * *

Ovid in the *Fasti* wages a *pitched battle* between order and chaos says the classicist Barbara Weiden Boyd. She discerns patterns in the seemingly unrelated episodes that *keep sending us back, inviting us to make new connections between previously unconnected phenomena.*

Ladies' botanies keep sending readers back to the link between women and flowers: *They too have their caprices and whims . . . some coquettish corollas vary their dress three times in a single day.* From the Sanskrit for "to burn."

> *An ordinary fire*
> *come to perch.*

Flora has magic that can make Juno pregnant, but she is unable to speak: *Thrice did I wish to promise help, but thrice my tongue was tied: the anger of great Jupiter filled me with fear.*

Juno reads the truth on Flora's face. She promises to keep Flora's name a secret, and the flower goddess agrees to make her pregnant:

> "Thy wish will be accomplished by a flower that was sent me
> from the fields of Olenus. He who gave it to me said, 'Touch
> also with this a barren heifer; she will be a mother.' I touched,
> and without delay she was a mother." Straightway I plucked
> with my thumb the clinging flower and touched Juno, and she
> conceived when it touched her bosom.

> touch which
>
>   doesn't speak   *come thumb*
>
> to swell the belly   dreamed I
>
>   spilled a lot of water on the floor
>
> and all the saints turned from me   I am the *no*
>
>   and the *yes* the flesh
>
> of the plum with no name   war breath

Dr. Weidon Boyd is professor of classics at Bowdoin, Cleaveland's alma mater. Say "nourishing mother."

* * *

First Strike

Force 2

Forest

Freedom

Frog Bam

Frontier

People living in the mountain valleys of New Guinea developed agriculture ten thousand years ago—possibly before Egypt and Mesopotamia. Outsiders weren't even aware of these communities until the 1920s, when Australian gold prospectors encountered close to a million people living in scattered highland villages.

The island has one of the most diverse bird populations on the planet, including most bird of paradise species ("a kind of seeing, an instance of sight"). Hunters nearly wiped out some species during the nineteenth century for feathers to adorn hats and dresses in London, Paris, and New York.

The economies of colonial Dutch and German New Guinea depended on the plume trade. To feed expanding industries at home, they exploited the island's other natural resources—timber, copper, gold, oil. The U.S. State Department notes that foreign investors continue to dominate these industries. Most of the population lives off subsistence farming.

As goddess of fertility, Flora protects the commons and the harvest they provide to the poor through nature's promiscuous bounty. *Honey is my gift,* she tells Ovid. *'Tis I who call the winged creatures.*

Ovid reports that before the gods brought the tools for agriculture, humans subsisted on acorns, *and the sturdy oak afforded a splendid affluence.*

> *Give me the eye to see a navy in an acorn,* wrote Emerson.

The word means "fruit of the unenclosed land," available to everyone.

* * *

In Paris, Emerson made little mention of the political turmoil that enveloped Grandville and so many others during this period, which Parisians called *the time of riots*. Emerson found Paris *a loud, modern New York of a place*. He took refuge in the Cabinet of Natural History with its formal gardens and cases of anatomical preparations—all of nature categorized according to the latest science.

The new classification system improved on Linnaeus by revealing hidden connections: each species, before seemingly isolated and random, was related to every other. Wandering through the museum, Emerson experienced an ecstatic revelation. He sensed the continuity of life: *I feel the centipede in me*, he wrote. *Cayman, carp, eagle, and fox.*

Half a century earlier, at the public gardens in Palermo, the writer Goethe had a similar epiphany. After years of carefully studying plants in all stages of growth, Goethe realized, in a sudden flash of insight, that what we call "the leaf" is the essential organ of the plant. Present in the seed, this bit of tissue contains nodes, or "eyes," through which it transforms to fulfill every function—calyx, petal, pistil. Instead of discrete parts, the plant consists of this single substance constantly transforming itself.

Emerson returned from Europe without a home, without a career, struggling to be a writer and comparing himself unfavorably to Shakespeare. But he carried the inspiration of the museum with him, and, influenced by Goethe, he comforted himself that even magnificent works must grow from small beginnings: *Every leaf contains the eyes which are sufficient to originate a forest.*

Louis Philippe, the "citizen king," pledged to uphold the French constitution, which mandated freedom of speech. The monarchy justified censoring the caricaturists by asserting that drawings went beyond speech by *speaking to the eyes*.

> *the horse of disaster*
> *rides inside a blank sky*

To destroy the jungle that blinded them, U.S. soldiers sprayed more than ten million gallons of Agent Orange on Vietnam. The chemicals spur rapid division in plant cells that function like stem cells in humans, transforming into many types of tissue. Unable to sustain the uncontrolled growth of leaves, stems, and shoots, the plant quickly blackens and dies all the way to the root.

* * *

Sometimes I see nothing in the cemetery. It is late August, afternoon, oppressive. I'm walking out, having completed the circuit of each of the lakes. Not even the egret is fishing in this heat. I pass a lone groundskeeper whacking weeds. He cuts the engine for me and waves. I wave back. In the quiet, no birds sing, only cicadas sparking from tree to tree—their sound seeming to thicken the humidity.

Then something growls, loud and low, right in my ear. I can almost feel it. I spin around, every hair electric. Nothing but hazy trees, the green starting his engine up a hundred yards off. I keep looking, trying to press my eyes through thick air. Something must be there, my heart pounding so hard I feel hollow, chemicals cascading through me—one nerve, one muscle. Ready.

But nothing breaks the surface of day, not even a leaf betrays the stillness. I turn back around, legs weak and palms aching from the rush of adrenaline. Cicadas. The engine. One worker. Me, and a countless crowd of bones covered by grass and soil.

what war
here forms
the surface for

* * *

Les Fleurs Animées insists on the link between gardening and motherhood—plants also demand *maternal tenderness and care.* But life givers can easily become killers: *However tender your feelings—however gentle those fair hands—the slightest inattention may compel you to reproach yourself with the death of these frail infants.*

From the Latin "unable to speak."

The first bird of paradise skins came to Europe aboard the Victoria in 1522, the only one of Magellan's ships to survive the first trip around the globe. The desire for more skins drew explorers to New Guinea. Since trade skins had neither legs nor wings, the myth spread that the birds descended from heaven and floated in air on their elaborate plumes, never touching earth until they died.

Green-Wood is one vast nursery, in which cribs give place to little caskets and coffins, and no one is afraid to speak loud lest they wake up the silent sleepers wrote the Rev. Theodore Cuyler, father of PRECIOUS GEORGIE. Everywhere, little doves and sleeping angels dissolve into grass—evidence that during the nineteenth century children died by the thousands. In one week during the summer of 1876, more than a hundred infants died every day, causing the *New York Times* to bemoan *the annual slaughter.*

So much death bewildered doctors. Reformers considered the loss of innocents a sign of moral decay brought on by the excesses of the new industrial economy. They laid the blame on mothers—wealthy women smothered their children with luxuries while the poor let their babies die from callous neglect. Either way, children came to be seen as inherently fragile, beings caught between this world and another. At any moment, greedy death might come to snatch the child back.

In the New Guinea highlands a group of people called Gimi believe that male children come from birds—they transform into humans from flying things. Another myth says that birds came from the body of a dead boy stored in a tree, and they were set free by a woman. During the rite of initiation into manhood, a boy transforms for an instant back into a bird of paradise and fuses with the spirits of his ancestors.

The doctor says he doesn't need the x-rays of my fallopian tubes and hands them back to me. In the absolute dark of my pelvis, the liquid curls like two ghost question marks.

I was always dead, weren't you?

* * *

Gangster

Gaucho

Genesis

Gladiator

Green Death

The industrial revolution transformed nineteenth-century Paris. Rural immigrants flooded the city, doubling its population. Lodging houses, workshops, and factories overflowed the medieval streets. Against this backdrop, Dumas wrote his novel *The Mohicans of Paris*. In Balzac's *Old Goriot*, one character declares: *Paris, you see, is like a forest in the New World where a score of savage tribes, the Illinois, the Hurons, struggle for existence.*

Inside this immense forest, it is impossible to see far through the vegetation, wrote the anthropologist Edward Schieffelin of the New Guinea jungle in the 1980s. *An outsider without a compass or a river to guide him can easily get disoriented and lost in the vast anonymity of trees.*

More than one hundred years earlier, in 1858, the English naturalist Alfred Russel Wallace described his first view of New Guinea:

> I looked with intense interest on those rugged mountains, retreating ridge behind ridge into the interior, where the foot of civilized man had never trod . . . Those dark forests produced the most extraordinary and the most beautiful of the feathered inhabitants of the earth—the varied species of the Birds of Paradise.

Paradise comes from ancient Iran, a compound of *pairi-* "around" + *diz* "to make or form (a wall)."

> *just to make, or shape, a body, and have it breathe like that*

In European tradition, only men wore feathers. Then one evening in 1775, on a whim, Marie Antoinette adorned her hair with ostrich and peacock plumes, and the king admired them. That started the trend among women. Peacock feathers went out of fashion after the French Revolution when the Queen was guillotined, but with the Restoration plumes returned to vogue.

Fashion . . . couples the living body to the inorganic world (Walter Benjamin). *To the living, it defends the rights of the corpse.*

* * *

Nearly a century before Emerson arrived in Paris, Linnaeus relied on preserved skins to describe the bird of paradise and assign it a scientific name (he called it *apoda*, "legless"). But it was only a few years before Emerson's visit that a naturalist encountered a living bird in the jungle. The French scientist René P. Lesson wrote *the gun remained idle in my hand for I was too astonished to shoot. It was in the virgin forest . . . like a meteor whose body, cutting through the air, leaves a long trail of light.*

the useless   a fire

Goethe referred to his revelation in the garden at Palermo as a *pregnant point*. Such moments depend on sight: The actual eye observes the world, and the inner mind's eye processes those impressions. The two kinds of sight fertilize a moment of knowledge that *bears many fruits*.

Neil Smith calls the concept of nature *sodden* with metaphor—usually female.

The animal becomes its own language.

The eye is formed by the light for the light so that the inner light may meet the outer wrote Goethe. He composed his *Metamorphosis of Plants* based on his insight at Palermo in part to counter the Linnaean classification, which relied on an abstract logic not intrinsic to the plants themselves.

There . . . arose a hunger in the lives of these people to impose order, to fix meaning, to arbitrate in the midst of chaos writes sociologist Richard Sennett of nineteenth-century Parisians. French realists helped serve this function. In their novels, the *flaneur* roams the city and catalogs its "types." The drawings of Grandville, Daumier, and others also popularized stock characters—the banker, the dandy, the laborer—that people could "read" like signposts in the wilderness. (*The flaneur goes botanizing on the asphalt*, wrote Benjamin.)

Gimi of the past considered the forest a male space, an *'exalted domain' of unlimited power where past, present and future intertwine to make the world and all the people in it*, says the anthropologist Paige West. Now that Christianity has become widespread, more and more Gimi believe it was God who created the forest instead of the forest that created them.

The Gimi word *Iuna* refers to an image that is in the mind but that is not visual and does not come from words—a feeling.

* * *

France's Cabinet of Natural History led the world in the effort to collect and classify all life forms on the planet. Founded as the king's private garden, it was nearly destroyed along with all the other trappings of royal privilege during the Reign of Terror.

But the cabinet's champions argued that it really belonged to the French people. As a national museum, it could help achieve the goals of the Revolution, transforming Frenchmen into sovereign citizens by providing them *a space outside space*, a refuge in which to contemplate the vast order of nature, and their place, like Adam, above it.

In Vietnam, the Demilitarized Zone and the mountain border with Laos contain much of the country's remaining forest, as well as birds, reptiles, and mammals never before encountered by scientists. Three decades of war kept people out of these regions. Some heavily bombed and mined areas remain too dangerous even to enter, and many trees can't be safely cut for timber because their trunks contain so much shrapnel.

Wallace, the nineteenth-century naturalist, had some of his best collecting success in places where trees were being cut. In Borneo, Chinese laborers felled the forest for a coal mine and railroad, attracting beetles to the dead and dying trees. Wallace collected an average of twenty-four new species every day for two weeks.

In this region, Wallace also shot fifteen orangutans. He kept a baby he had orphaned (it clung to his beard), but it grew more and more sick from lack of milk. After three months of studying it and enjoying the *daily amusement* it provided, he killed it, skinned it, and preserved it along with the others. (He never identifies its sex.)

The Cabinet of Natural History depended on violence for its collections. It confiscated the private cabinets of wealthy families killed or exiled by the Revolution and ransacked the collections of European monarchs defeated by Revolutionary Armies. Even the serene rationality the museum projected was an illusion: It displayed species using contradictory classification systems because its officials couldn't agree on the proper order of nature.

literally "birth," from *natus*, "the result of being born."

Havahart

Heavy Weight

Helena

Hercules

Heritage

Home Best

* * *

The philodendron I got as a gift starts to turn yellow. I think maybe it needs a new pot, so I walk to McGovern Florist, the weathered building with the glass cupola across the street from Green-Wood. The decaying glass building looks like something dropped out of a fairytale between the gas station and an old row house. Local legend says it came from the 1904 St. Louis World's Fair.

The old building creaks, and so does its owner. She stoops and searches, but finds no pots. In fact, the greenhouse is almost entirely bare. The funeral business is down, she explains: *People used to have three-day wakes, and everybody wanted mounds of flowers. Now the undertakers pick up a body and put it in the ground the same day.*

Her young grandson sits in a wheelchair beside her, a cast on his foot. I want to know what happened. *I hugged a tombstone,* he says, with some pride. She nods: *Freak accident. It fell right down on him. We go over all the time to see Nana. I don't know why this time he wanted to hug the thing.*

Back home, without a pot, I try pinching the yellow leaves off. Every stem I pull out is covered in tiny white insects. I look close, the whole plant crawls with them—flat, round mealybugs—their sharp mouths sucking out sap. The ones crushed by my fingers leave a white dust on my hands. Disgusted, I toss the whole plant in the trash.

* * *

Of course, it wasn't really greedy death that caused so many children to die during the nineteenth century. It was greedy people. Industrialists got rich off new arrivals pouring into the cities for low-paying wage work. Landlords earned huge rents by cramming people into tenements where backyard toilets overflowed and garbage rotted in the streets.

How soon one feels as if one is suffocating in these dark, narrow, and damp thoroughfares that are known simply as the streets of Paris! declared one writer for the popular papers. *And thousands of people live, bustle, throng in the damp darkness like reptiles in a swamp.*

(Swamp comes from North America. Captain John Smith first used it in 1624 to describe the landscape of Virginia.)

To depict life in the city, realist writers emulated the methods of naturalists. Balzac promoted his *Human Comedy* as the sociological equivalent of the Cabinet of Natural History. He came up with the idea for a comprehensive study of Parisian society while wandering around the museum the same summer that Emerson was there.

The displays that inspired Balzac and Emerson had little in common with the original animal. Shells, beaks, bones, and skin were easiest to preserve, and most specimens consisted only of these hard tissues. Brains, hearts, and other organs could not be represented, nor could the bodies of more fragile creatures.

Wallace felt this loss. He described capturing a bird-winged butterfly in New Guinea:

> I trembled with excitement as I saw it coming majestically toward me, and could hardly believe I had really succeeded in my stroke till I had taken it out of the net and was gazing, lost in admiration, at the velvet black and brilliant green of its wings, seven inches across, its golden body, and crimson breast. It is true I had seen similar insects in cabinets, at home, but it is quite another thing to capture such one's self—to feel it struggling between one's fingers, and to gaze upon its fresh and living beauty, a bright gem shining out amid the silent gloom of a dark and tangled forest.

New Yorkers at first refused to bury their dead in Green-Wood, which they considered wild land, unprotected. They *clung to the charnel-house and churchyard* wrote Cleaveland. So the trustees erected an obelisk over an empty grave to act *as a sort of decoy.*

From the Dutch for "cage"—it referred to the practice of capturing water birds by surrounding a pond with nets.

* * *

To speak about the structure of lament, Kaluli in New Guinea use metaphors of water. The rainforest that surrounds them drips, and so do the sounds they make. The song pours over a ledge, rushes downwards, and levels off into a still pool. It plunges again like a waterfall, or it splits, some sounds remaining high on the land while others drop. Sounds stream, swirl, flow, and splash.

The early church father St. Gregory of Nyssa also favored water metaphors. One scholar calls his writing *well irrigated*. In his treatise *On Virginity*, he contrasts the *still pool* of self-control with the *crashing waves of feeling* the body gives rise to. He compares virginity to strong walls that channel the stream and prevent it from spilling over the land.

But it is the virgins he so admired who cause the saint to lose control. The nuns break out into wailing at the death of Gregory's older sister, their mother superior. Gregory writes: *My reason no longer maintained itself, but, like a mountain stream overflowing, it was overwhelmed below the surface by my suffering, and, disregarding the tasks at hand, I gave myself wholly over to lamentation.*

In Green-Wood, the seasonal ponds, which local farmers called "collects," proved to be the landscape's most unruly feature: "unable to be controlled by the stick or rule."

> *Of persons. Of animals. Of heart, tongue, passions.*

Cleaveland quotes from the report on the effort to *improve these little lakes:*

> Their borders were graded and shaped, covered with verdure, and shaded with appropriate foliage. It soon appeared that they were liable to changes, which marred their beauty, or even made them offensive . . . the exhalations from their desiccated beds were disagreeable and unwholesome.

St. Gregory recovered himself and ordered the nuns out of the death chamber. But the virgins kept coming back and erupting into lament. Finally, the church officials just proceeded with the funeral, attempting to drown them out.

The Kaluli traditionally held a week-long ceremony of weeping. They hung the body in loops and placed a basin underneath in case it dripped. But Christianity has become widespread among the villages, and the missionaries frown on such displays. Now most mourners cut the weeping short and "plant" the body quickly in the soil.

* * *

Collecting rare plants and animals for scientific study overlapped with their collection for commerce and empire. Naturalists competed for the best specimens, and local traders took advantage of this. The Dutch colonist van Duivenboden and his sons made a fortune acquiring bird of paradise skins and selling them to the highest bidder.

The American W.F. Alder described one method for obtaining the birds: First, local hunters build a blind in the "dancing tree"—where the birds return every year for mating. The males descend and unfurl their bright plumage, while females fill the surrounding trees to watch.

> The birds become so engrossed in their strutting and vain showing-off to the females that the hunters are able to shoot them down one by one . . . Frequently the hunters . . . kill two thirds of the birds before the others take alarm and fly away.

As exotic species poured in, a *vogue for the natural sciences* gripped both sides of the Atlantic. Residents of London and Paris flocked to the museums, and Emerson gave his first lectures on *Nature* before eager Boston audiences. The new science offered spectacle—a glimpse of the remote and bizarre. But it also promised to make sense of the world, bringing all species—the familiar and the strange—together under a single, rational system. Natural history provided a comforting sense of order to nineteenth-century urban dwellers, while all around them *social orders shifted and collapsed.*

Grandville's most fantastic book, *Un Autre Monde,* published in 1844, captures the sense of a world turned upside down: Smiling fish lure humans from the water with jewels, money, and alcohol, and an orchestra of steam-powered machines play themselves. A hobgoblin wandering lost through the universe finds the Milky Way paved for ease of travel and Saturn's ring transformed into an iron balcony for enjoying the view.

In the *Arcades Project*, Walter Benjamin calls Grandville the *tribal sorcerer* and credits him with first capturing the essence of the commodity, with its *luster of distraction.*

At his 1855 dedication of Sleepy Hollow, the garden cemetery in Concord, Emerson declared *When I think of . . . the speed of the changes of that glittering dream we call existence,—I think sometimes that the vault of the sky . . . is only a Sleepy Hollow, with path of Suns, instead of foot-paths; and Milky Ways, for truck-roads.*

* * *

Wallace did not find the birds of paradise he had hoped for along the coast of New Guinea. He soon realized that many species lived far inland, in the mountains, and came through trade to coastal villages. West, the anthropologist, points out that the highlands Wallace imagined as *trackless wilds* had been connected to international trading networks for thousands of years.

Wildlife markets in Vietnam recently provided scientists with their first glimpse of several "new" species, such as the Annamite striped rabbit. The markets thrive in most cities and towns, feeding an illegal global animal trade that in size follows only drugs and guns. Vendors sell a wide array of live creatures, from geckoes to orangutans, as well as stuffed skins, and parts used for traditional medicine: tiger bones, bear bile, deer antlers *(especially immature ones covered in velvet)*, and rhinoceros horns.

For centuries, insects plagued animal collectors. Beetles could devour an entire cabinet of skins within a few hours. Then in the early nineteenth century, a taxidermist at the Paris museum discovered that arsenic would kill insects without destroying the specimen. Embalmers also began to use the chemical. Arsenic preserved the body and left it flexible, so that it could be dressed and posed in a way that mimicked life.

I drew in your last breath with my mouth, that I might share your death, wrote St. Ambrose of his beloved older brother Satyrus. In his funeral address, the fourth-century church father veers from cries of lament to condemning grief as *soft and effeminate,* the mark of an unbeliever. He also used the occasion to reprove female mourners:

> They affect soiled garments, as if there were a feeling of grief in these. They wet their disheveled hair with filth. Finally, what seems to be in vogue in many localities, they rend their mantles, tear open their garments, and make a public display of their nakedness . . . thus they invite wanton eyes to lust after those naked limbs.

Linnaeus assigned orangutans the scientific name *satyrus* because of their popular association with satyrs—the lustful, debauched creatures of myth.

In medieval bestiaries, Satyrus was the name of a female ape that always gave birth to twins. She cradled the one she loved, while the one she hated had to cling to her back. In some stories, she drops the beloved child to escape a hunter, and the despised child on her back lives. In others, she smothers the beloved in her arms.

* * *

Imperial
Impact Zone
Instant Frog
Intruder
Invader
Island Breeze

Wallace had better luck on Waigeo, an island off the northwest coast of
New Guinea: Local hunters brought him several birds of paradise still alive.
He tried keeping them in bamboo cages, feeding them fruit and insects, but,
he wrote, *on the morning of the third day they were almost always found dead at
the bottom of the cage, without any apparent cause.*

The historian Anne Larsen explains the process of preserving them:

> Once the bird was dead, all the orifices and the wounds had to be
> carefully stopped up with cotton to prevent the feathers from being
> soiled; it was then placed head downward in a paper cone that kept
> it clean and immobile . . . Ornithologists collecting in the tropics
> had to act within a few hours to preserve birds against scavenging
> insects and putrefaction by skinning them and preparing the clean
> skin with a heavy dose of pesticide.

In eight years traveling the Malay Archipelago, Wallace collected more than
125,000 birds, beetles, shells, butterflies, and mammals. He and his servants
spent much of their time skinning, pinning, and preserving. Sometimes
insects and other scavengers got to the specimens anyway. On the island of
Lombok, Wallace placed the legs of the skinning bench in coconut shells
filled with water to keep out the ants, which swarmed over everything. In
Borneo, dogs carried off almost an entire orangutan.

Orangutan in Malay means "man of the woods," but it did not refer to the
animal. Residents of Java may have originally used the word to describe forest
tribes they considered savage. European cultures shared a similar myth:
Dangerous, man-like creatures lived in the woods, *all chasers and rapists of women.*

Linnaeus ignited a storm of controversy when he placed the orangutan in
the same genus as humans. The Count de Buffon, Linneaus' adversary, ran
the Cabinet of Natural History when it was still the Garden of the King.
He proclaimed that orangutans might *wear a human mask*, but they differed
fundamentally from humans because of something invisible—the soul.

* * *

93

Victorians expressed their enthusiasm for natural history by taking up botany, which did not require *chasing or killing animals*.

> (From the Latin, "a being that breathes.")

Listen

One hundred years after Wallace tramped through the forests of Borneo shooting orangutans, another young scientist came to save them. Biruté Galdikas was one of the "angels"—along with Dian Fossey and Jane Goodall—recruited by the anthropologist Louis Leakey to conduct the first long-term studies of great apes in their native habitats. Galdikas also began taking in young orangutans captured for the illegal pet trade—many had been violently orphaned, their mothers shot out from under them.

In her autobiography *Reflections of Eden*, Galdikas writes:

> Instinctively, as a female primate, I provided the maternal environment for the . . . orangutans who became members of my forest family . . . I hugged, carried, caressed, and loved them. They became addicted to me and I to them. Their physical warmth, their soft squeals, their expressions, their feel became part of my daily life in the forest. . . . They weren't human but they were close enough.

* * *

Victorians found many uses for arsenic besides preserving bodies. It produced a brilliant green dye that became the color of choice for fabric and wallpaper. It appeared in cookware, floor cleaner, even candy. Despite the fact that arsenic is lethal in tiny amounts, Victorians drank it as a tonic for fevers and skin problems. Women took arsenic to increase their breast size.

Grandville's drawings of flowers transformed into women appeared in 1847. *Les Fleurs Animées* achieved instant popularity, with a second edition printed the same year. Cleaveland's English translation quickly followed, as did Belgian and German editions. Grandville didn't get to enjoy this success— he died earlier that year in an insane asylum and was buried outside Paris in the cemetery of Saint Mandé.

Garden cemeteries weren't for the dead only. They provided a place for the living to contemplate death in a setting that recalled Eden. More practically, in the era before public parks, cemeteries offered a refuge from the city. Manhattanites crowded onto the Brooklyn ferry and flowed through Green-Wood's gates to picnic and lounge throughout the grounds. The cemetery developed into a must-see tourist attraction.

In Borneo, Galdikas recalled an idyllic afternoon at her research station in the jungle, sitting beneath the jackfruit trees, one orangutan infant asleep on her shoulder, one sitting beside her, and one snoozing on the table in front of her. *I felt to the marrow of my bones and to the depths of my soul that the apes surrounding me were refugees from paradise, a paradise that we humans left behind . . . These apes were survivors of Eden.*

(Survivors "of" not "from"

as if it had been a war.)

In 1844, Walt Whitman wrote for the New York *Sunday Times* about a visit to Green-Wood: *In driving quietly through the grounds, we surprised a young couple who appeared to be making love. We laughed outright, not withstanding the sacredness of the place.*

from the root *saq*, "to bind, enclose, restrict"

Galdikas appeared on the cover of *National Geographic* in October 1975, a radiant young woman with long flowing hair, an orangutan toddler clinging to her hand, and an infant balanced on her hip, tugging on her loose, low-cut shirt.

* * *

Throughout his life, Benjamin felt haunted by a *little hunchback* (an echo of Grandville's lost hobgoblin?) He feared that *the little man, by looking at you* would bring misfortune.

In Grandville's *Venus at the Opera* a languid looking woman floats in a theatre box above the crowd, which consists of eyeballs. They swivel inside their wrinkled lids to stare at her—the gaze personified.

He seems to see out of every pore of his skin, Emerson wrote about Goethe.

The German writer's influence radiated through both Emerson and Benjamin. Each focused on the minuscule as a container or concentration of the whole, hoping to encounter in the small and minute not just emblems or symbols but an actual instance of the all in concentrated form—as Benjamin wrote, *the crystal of the total event.*

This kind of investigation required the techniques of natural history. Benjamin treated nineteenth-century commodities as fossils that contained the clues to the present. Emerson penetrated the recesses of his darkest moments the way the anatomist probed the interior of the animal body, purifying them into written specimens.

The dissection/preservation method of science renders everything visible to the eye, writes Brown, the Emerson scholar. *Composition, like natural history, aims to keep what it transforms; and in curing its materials of mortal idiosyncrasy, it must turn to techniques comparable to those of taxidermy.*
(literally "to arrange the skin")

The fact that arsenic was cheap and easily available led to widespread anxiety about poisonings. Newspapers published lurid accounts of such murders—they usually featured women from the lower classes slipping arsenic into food to kill their husbands and children.

In 2008, scientists analyzed photos of New Guinea taken by satellite *(the eye is the first circle)*. The images revealed more rapid logging than anyone had previously realized. They concluded that within thirteen years, most of the country's forests would be damaged or destroyed completely.

* * *

Grandville transformed all of nature into a commodity and ended in madness, wrote Benjamin. Both men died in their forties, almost exactly a hundred years apart, both driven to their deaths by the Paris of modernity— in Benjamin's case, Paris the nightmare city in the hands of the Nazis.

Balzac compared Paris to a vast ocean: *Sound it: you will never touch bottom. Survey it, report on it! However scrupulous your survey and reports, however numerous and persistent the explorers of this sea may be, there will always remain virgin places, undiscovered caverns, flowers, pearls, monsters.*

(From the root *monere* "to warn.") Medieval Europeans believed that malformed animals signaled impending disaster.

After he fled Berlin, the city of his birth, Benjamin wrote:
Your heart beats louder and louder and louder,
The sea grows quieter and quieter and quieter
To the very depths.

Evil slithered inside the Eden that Galdikas built. She admits toward the end of her book that she suspected her first and favorite child, Sugito, of *drowning one and possibly two* other orangutan children. And a nearly full-grown ex-captive named Gundul raped an Indonesian woman, a cook working at the camp.

Galdikas witnessed the attack and tried in vain to fight the orangutan off:

> The cook stopped struggling. "It's all right," she murmured. She lay back in my arms, with Gundul on top of her. Gundul was very calm and deliberate . . . . he moved rhythmically back and forth, his eyes rolled upward to the heavens.

Galdikas records the name of the animal, but not the woman. We hear none of her words beyond *It's all right.* Galdikas does report the husband's reaction: *It was just an ape. Why should my wife or I be concerned? It wasn't a man.*

Reflections of Eden includes a picture of Galdikas with Gundul. In the closely cropped photo, Galdikas faces the lens, looking down at the animal with a slightly furrowed brow. Gundul sits in profile, also looking down, his eye a pool of shadow.

* * *

The United States used arsenic to destroy rice crops in the Mekong Delta. Its code name was Agent Blue. The same arsenic-based herbicide became the chemical of choice for killing weeds at home.

In 2009, the government reached a voluntary agreement with the manufacturers to phase out arsenic-based pesticides because of concerns about the poison in drinking water. At the time, the chemical appeared in more than two hundred products. See, for example:

Adios

Aristocrat

Good-life

Lawn a magic

Red panther

Wondergro

The Mekong River changes names several times along its 2,700 miles. At its origin in the Tibetan Himalayas it is called *Dza Chu*, Water of Stone. In China's Yunnan Province, it is *Lancang Jiang*, Turbulent River. In Thai it is *Mae Nam Khong*, Mother River. At its delta, the Mekong drains into the East Sea through nine mouths, the source of its Vietnamese name, *Song Cuu Long*, or the River of Nine Dragons.

Dragon comes from the Greek verb "to see clearly." *But perhaps the literal sense is "the one with the (deadly) glance."*

Wallace tried often to keep animals alive. He almost always failed. During four years in Brazil he collected around a hundred live animals, but by the time he prepared to sail for London, only thirty-four remained: *five monkeys, two macaws, twenty parrots or paroquets, a white-crested pheasant, some small birds, and his favorite, a fully grown and very tame toucan.* The night before Wallace sailed, the toucan flew overboard and drowned.

Then, in the middle of the ocean, Wallace's ship caught fire. He escaped to a small boat with the other passengers and watched the ship burn: *Some of the parrots and monkeys retreated to the bowsprit, and as it caught fire, they ran back, and disappeared in the flames.*

* * *

Mass production alienated Grandville from his own work. Engravers prepared his drawings for printing, and he was often unsatisfied with the product. In the contract for the book on flowers, he agreed to sign his name to drawings produced by other artists, *humiliating terms* that one critic suggested had to do with Grandville's despair over the deaths of his first wife and most of his children.

By the 1970s, supplies of rot-resistant American trees like redwood and cedar had become scarce. Timber companies met the continuing demand for cheap lumber by cutting less hardy Ponderosa pine and Douglas fir. To preserve this wood so that it wouldn't rot, they injected it with arsenic.

About 70% of American homes have decks or porches made from arsenic-treated wood, says the chemist William Cullen. Regular wood needs to be replaced every few years, but lumber preserved with arsenic lasts up to six decades. A single backyard deck requires about three 45-year-old trees. Because of this, the industry says that using arsenic in wood protects the forest.

More than three decades after the war, the land in Vietnam remains bare in many places. Some areas have been colonized by aggressive species of weeds known as *American grass.*

In his final work, Grandville's earlier satirical sharpness has softened into what the collector Peter Wick calls flowers in *haute couture.*

Parisian women, in turn, echoed plants: After the revolution of 1830, dresses in France grew *fuller and more flower shaped.* Fashion houses also remained fixated on feathers. Bird plumes cascaded from hats, gowns, capes, and parasols. The trimmings grew more and more excessive: By the end of the century, hats commonly sported entire birds, and dress hems trailed *swallows' wings, downy tufts of marabou and glossy-smooth grebe skins*—even, in one case, finch heads.

In the *Arcades Project* section on "Fashion," Benjamin suggests that, since *the horizontal positioning of the body* is best during pregnancy, women at first did not walk erect. *The woman would have been the four-footed companion of the man,* he writes. Face-to-face intercourse he imagines as a kind of *deviance* through which women learned to walk upright.

* * *

Kaput
Kill Zone
Konk
Labyrinth
Lariat
Leisure Time

The doctor concludes that nothing is wrong with me, except, of course, for the fact that I am female, and so is my partner. Our sperm arrives by FedEx, purchased frozen from a far away bank.

> (Sperm and speech intertwine—both come from the root word "to scatter.")

Wallace became obsessed with the idea of bringing living birds of paradise home with him. The creatures could carry the wild world into the gloom of Victorian London. If he could sell them to the new Zoological Society, they might also provide financial security for the rest of his life.

On February 6, 1862, Wallace bought two lesser birds of paradise from a trader in Singapore for £92 (around $400—he talked the seller down from $500). During the long journey home, he fed the birds cockroaches he caught in the ship's storeroom and bought them fruit at every stop. He also sent off a stream of telegrams to London—he worried that the birds might die in the cold weather, and he wanted to sell them as soon as possible.

In 1983, a U.S. Forest Service worker in Indiana sawed picnic tables out of arsenic-treated wood and began vomiting blood. A woman in Salt Lake City got slivers of Douglas fir in her hand and had to have her fingers cut off. After several such incidents, the timber industry agreed in 2002 to stop using arsenic in wood for residential use. The millions of tons of arsenic-laden wood nationwide qualify as hazardous waste, but the government created a special exemption so that it could go into regular garbage dumps.

In the Gimi language, the term *neki maha* means "crazy ground" or "mad ground," says West, the anthropologist. Traditionally, it referred to dangerous places in the forest, where no one hunted or gathered. The souls of the unborn and young children who had died tended to gather in these places. A man who trespassed here might bring harmful consequences to his wife and children, even those not yet born. *The neki maha was also used metaphorically by men to describe the dangerous interior of women's bodies.*

* * *

The London Zoo staged a festive reception for Wallace's birds of paradise, a *brilliant addition to their collection,* and housed them in a new aviary, right at the entrance gate. Wallace received £150 for the birds—a £58 profit. He notes that they lived for one and two years, respectively.

Grandville wrote his own epitaph, though it doesn't seem to appear on his grave: *Here lies Grandville; he gave life to everything and made everything move and speak. The one thing is, he didn't know how to make his own way.*

Lisa Fittko crossed the Pyrenees with Benjamin to escape the Nazis the night he killed himself. The next day, the guards allowed the rest of the refugees to cross. In 1980, Fittko wrote down her memories of "Old Benjamin": *What a strange man. A crystal-clear mind; unbending inner strength; yet, a wooly-headed bungler.*

In the introduction to *Illuminations,* Hannah Arendt wrote that Benjamin *was of course speaking about himself when . . . he quoted what Jacques Rivière had said about Proust: he 'died of the same inexperience that permitted him to write his works. He died of ignorance . . . because he did not know how to make a fire or open a window.'*

Fittko reports that Benjamin struggled to carry a large black briefcase that he said contained his new manuscript. *Under no circumstances would he part with his ballast, that black bag,* she wrote. *We would have to drag the monster across the mountains.* The briefcase has since been lost.

After his death, Grandville's wife and eldest son, disturbed by his drawings, destroyed them. Prints from his books still sell online for hundreds of dollars. At the library, I have to promise not to take photos.

Benjamin died poor. His grave at Portbou is not marked.

In March 2009, the press reported that scientists encountered fifty-six new species *in the teeming virgin tropical forests of Papua New Guinea.* The two-month expedition uncovered dozens of new jumping spiders, three new frogs, and a striped gecko. News stories refer to the jungle as a *Lost World* and a *rich hunting ground.* The animals are pictured alive.

* * *

Liberator

Lifegard

Miracle

Mosquito Deleto

Motherearth

I haven't set foot in Green-Wood for more than nine months. I live now
2,449 miles away in Portland, Oregon—another edge place, carved by water.

By chance I rent a house near the city's oldest cemetery. I visit and learn its
contours. I take a tour. I listen to the stories. But it doesn't hold me. I spend
my time on my knees in the yard with my hands in the landlord's dirt. I jab
a trowel in and watch the earthworms recoil. I crumble soil and smell its
bacterial funk. I wake every morning thinking about things growing.

No.

That arc, it's fake. Nothing dies   not the years   fear
breathed me   no air   not the shiver
of impact, the plane through the body of the building
to the silver train in its burrow. The sound of that.

I came up, yes, like the myth, from under the earth
flames   paper as rain   a smell the brain contains
no name for. Diesel I guess. Steel, carpeting and
furniture, clothing, bones
                                        and skin also
nothing now   breathed in.

I didn't breathe. No. I'd like to say so. A sort of
scorched awake   wait   until you shimmer. I wanted
to "hold" that breath. I held you,
fear, like this: an infant at my breast   not killed
I kept you   not killed   no name   eat
dirt and melt. I wanted that.
                                        But breath

itself took over. Breathed me everyone
else's air like it might disappear. Breathed
like any animal panic
of oxygen-swelled blood and all it's pregnant with (see
"poisoned" in reference to)   quick
and warm like anyone   breathed.

The signs

still say years later *if you are sick*
you should tell someone. If you are sick you will not
be left alone on the train after
everyone else has run off. What made us move as if
one creature   the sound?
The shiver? (of unknown origin,
but the earlier verb means to break
into pieces, splinter).
Thus begins

our myth: Once upon
a climbing up, I didn't want to speak
or touch   walking uptown   strange in a strange
set of streets, newish to this most famous place (from the
Sanskrit for "to speak"). Then I heard a voice
from the radio (a word once used
only by soldiers). Not thinking I pierced
the city skin, put my sandaled foot with BLUE
MOON® toenails on the step of the delivery truck
and leaned my head in to listen: *towers . . . planes . . . the*
pentagon . . . so intoned an old ocean
engulfs me

Don't cry, says the guy at the wheel. *We'll bomb them*
off the face of the earth.
Slapped, I step back. Smelling blood
the excitement of that. I   l   I
I didn't want to be fucked like that, not to give birth

to rivers of blood. But I was. I did.
So I clamped my mouth shut around it. Right then.
It was done.

Thus, scorched inside I smoked and turned ghost.

No, that's Poetry-swagger, false, a cover like
the cemetery=sleep. For-real-fear small + ugly
became my blasted life and nothing would grow there.
Nothing would sleep.   I learned what lives
in the graveyard—trees—there
I could breathe.   I could choose to.   *Speak,*
she said, *from the trees' point of view.* But I'm cursed. I
didn't know how. I buried myself in dead trees instead.
Hardwood and softwood   aspen   birch   fir
and larch torn fiber from fiber   reborn monster-like
as books. *Look the creature speaks!*

Standing on my own throat my wooden
dummy croaks:
Paris a vast ocean
the cypress in Vietnam no scientist knew existed that sprouts out
of ancient corals its nearest relation the American nootka spruce
proof the land once connected in a single ocean that flooded
leaving 200-million-year-old-sediments-along-the-banks-of-
the-Mekong-with-its-many-names-which-stitches-six-
nations-but-no-one-completed-the-trip-from-mouth-to-
source-until-the-last-century-and-scientistsstilldisagreeaboutwhereexactlyit
springsfromtheearth.
                    Science from the root "to cut."

Like a good worker I produced, like a poet I put
things together. But my shaky edifice collapsed. I failed
to keep faith with facts. I just wanted them (to
splinter) to give up
their ghosts (that's rage, to tear apart). Truth
from the root "tree," think *solid as an oak.* You,

stupid word, dressed in a white
nothing
you'll fade to. You only can kill
out of mouths
or die.

That's not true either. It's the voice that demands a
body, unlike   thought   light   the first
that floods all form without end   Look.   It's nothing
the blank that shines off buildings & faces, sidewalks,
rivers, the dirt   all sight a form of blindness
                the eye
created by light for light that needs no body to move
through.   I knew this first as narrative's false fit
the need for the gap   breathe in
breathe out.

I wanted that blank   to wake up into it. But something
kept the flesh in its shape. Kept me breathing and
stoked the fucking pulse. Maybe the voice itself.

I dreamed I wrote for help on bits of my own skin
but was forced to eat them. Awake I ate myself
from the inside *pointed arches leaking sky.* Could I have
said the word sooner?
                Yes.   I said
yes and the yes turned to no—a scream.
But not futile, not
infertile as Emerson thought *just a stirring*
in the mud. That's the edge, living and dead
that gives birth, duh, to everything The scream
grew into ocean   the air   a thing I could breathe through
that breathed through me.

That fails. It's metaphor. But there is this fact.
Not fact, a sense, from to find one's way: a body
in pain   or joy   without thought   before

thought   wants to sound

                  resound. So I open my mouth

and become that breath-forced wail *common*
to many cultures, red muscle threads pumping, rib
bellows sounding the bone-bridged instrument I am—
chest hollow, throat tube, the holes
behind the face—not
history   the law   not comfort,
logic, or custom—not
poetry. I have
no ritual for this, no place
to exist. I grow strange, a cry
and nothing else, the force that
through the darkness moves the breath.
                                    I let it go

it comes back.

NOTES

The etymologies throughout the book come from the Oxford English Dictionary and from Douglas Harper's poetic and minutely researched dictionary at etymonline.com. The OED is expensive; Harper's web site is free, but users can support it by sponsoring a word.

PAGE 6

Henry Evelyn Pierrepont founder of Green-Wood:

- John Looby. "Virtual American Biographies." James Pierrepont. 2001. Accessed April 22, 2018. http://famousamericans.net/jamespierrepont/.
- Jeffrey I. Richman, *Brooklyn's Green-Wood Cemetery: New York's Buried Treasure* (Brooklyn: The Green-Wood Cemetery, 1998), 6, 8-9.
- Nehemiah Cleaveland, *Green-Wood Cemetery: A History of the Institution from 1838 to 1864*, (New York: Anderson & Archer, 1866), 6, 17.

PAGE 7-8

Trinity Church graveyard *saturated with . . . flesh*:

- Charles Shively, *A History of the Conception of Death in America, 1650-1860* (New York & London: Garland Publishing, Inc. 1988), 345.

Bones had to be dug up to make room for new bodies:

- James Stevens Curl, *The Victorian Celebration of Death* (Detroit: The Partridge Press, 1972), 170.
- *Brooklyn's Green-Wood Cemetery*, 4.

PAGE 9-10

William Niblo's grave:

- Cleaveland, *A Hand-book for Green-Wood* (New York: E.B. Tripp, 1878), 83-84.

Hunters nearly wiped out the egret:

- Joan Dunning, *Secrets of the Nest: The Family Life of North American Birds* (Boston: Houghton Mifflin Company, 1994), 63-66.

- William Souder, "How Two Women Ended the Deadly Feather Trade," *Smithsonian Magazine*, March 2013. Accessed April 22, 2018. https://www.smithsonianmag.com/science-nature/how-two-women-ended-the-deadly-feather-trade-23187277/

a kind of appetite, a trace:
- Lyn Hejinian, "Happily," *The Language of Inquiry* (Berkeley: University of California Press, 2000), 383-385.

Cemeteries as a place to sleep:
- *A History of the Conception of Death*, 343.
- *Brooklyn's Green-Wood Cemetery*, 4-5, 7.

Emerson's ecstatic vision:
- Robert D. Richardson, Jr., *Emerson: The Mind on Fire* (Berkeley: University of California Press, 1995), 162, 177.

PAGE 11
The Transcendentalists on cemeteries and nature:
- *Brooklyn's Green-Wood Cemetery*, 5-8
- Ralph Waldo Emerson, *Nature* in *The Complete Works of Ralph Waldo Emerson, Vol. 1 Nature, Addresses and Lectures* (New York: Houghton Mifflin, 1903-1904). Accessed April 22, 2018. https://quod.lib.umich.edu/e/emerson/4957107.0001.001/1:9?view=toc.

The population grew ten-fold during Emerson's lifetime:
- "U.S. Population, 1790-2000: Always Growing," United States History. Accessed April 22, 2018. http://www.u-s-history.com/pages/h980.html.
- Campbell Gibson and Kay Jung, "Historical Census Statistics On Population Totals By Race, 1790 to 1990, and By Hispanic Origin, 1970 to 1990, For Large Cities And Other Urban Places In The United States," U.S. Census Bureau, February 2005. Accessed April 22, 2018. https://www.census.gov/population/www/documentation/twps0076/twps0076.html

Ice from Walden Pond shipped to Calcutta:
- *Mind on Fire*, 381.

Forest and wildlife disappearing:
- David Wilcove, *The Condor's Shadow* (New York: W.H. Freeman and Company, 1999), 18-24.
- Michael Williams, *Americans and Their Forests* (Cambridge: Cambridge University Press, 1992), 193.

Rural cemeteries domesticate nature and death:
- *A History of the Conception of Death*, 348-366.
- *Brooklyn's Green-Wood Cemetery*, 4-8.

glad to the brink of fear:

- Emerson, *Nature*, Chapter 1.

PAGE 12

Cormorants dying:

- Glenn Martin, "Sea life in peril—plankton vanishing," *San Francisco Chronicle*, July 12, 2005, A1.

Susan Howe on libraries and cormorants:

- Susan Howe, *The Birth-mark: Unsettling the wilderness in American literary history* (Hanover, NH: Wesleyan University Press, 1993), 18, 26-30.

New York tries to eradicate cormorants:

- Lisa W. Foderaro, "Cormorants Take Over, Making Some Enemies," *The New York Times*, July 1, 2005, B1.
- "Double-crested Cormorant," NYS Dept. of Environmental Conservation. Accessed April 22, 2018. http://www.dec.ny.gov/animals/7065.html.

PAGE 13

Whitman in Green-Wood:

- Walt Whitman, *The Journalism in The Collected Writings of Walt Whitman, Vol. 1 1834-1846*, ed. Herbert Bergman (New York: Peter Lang, 1998), 9, 421.
- Whitman, *The Journalism, Vol. 2 1846-1848*, ed. Herbert Bergman (New York: Peter Lang, 2003), 277.
- Whitman, *Notebooks and Unpublished Prose Manuscripts, Volume IV: Notes*, ed. Edward F. Grier (New York: New York University Press, 1984), 1393.

1840s, Emerson and Brook Farm commune:

- *The Mind on Fire*, 340-346.

Green-Wood and security:

- *Green-Wood Cemetery: A History*, 26-27.
- *Green-Wood Cemetery Rules and Regulations*, 1849, 22.

PAGE 15

Nehemiah Cleaveland on fences:

- *Green-Wood Cemetery: A History*, 94 and 142.

PAGE 16

Brooklyn families sell out to the cemetery, but smaller owners refuse:

- *Green-Wood Cemetery: A History*, 8, 11, 13, 21.
- *Brooklyn's Green-Wood Cemetery*, 9.

PAGE 17

Ancient Saxon tribes carved runes in beech:

- Della Hook, *Trees in Anglo-Saxon England: Literature, Lore and Landscape* (Suffolk, UK: Boydell & Brewer, 2010).

- Elbert L. Little, *National Audubon Society Field Guide to North American Trees*, Eastern Region, (New York: Alfred A. Knopf, 1980), 382.

PAGE 18

The extent of the forest encountered by colonists:
- *Americans and Their Forests*, 3-5.
- Barbara Freese, *Coal: a Human History* (Cambridge, MA: Perseus Publishing, 2003), 104.

Colonists' attitudes toward the forest:
- *Americans and Their Forests*, 10-14, 60-67, 353-355.
- Simon Schama, *Landscape and Memory* (New York: Alfred A. Knopf, 1995), 1-19.
- Roderick Nash, *Wilderness and the American Mind*, (New Haven: Yale University Press, 1967), 8-22, 27.

Native societies shaped the landscape:
- *Americans and Their Forests*, 32-49, 57.
- James Wilson, *The Earth Shall Weep: A History of Native America*, (New York: Grove Press, 1998), 65-69.
- Charles C. Mann, *1491: New Revelations of the Americas Before Columbus* (New York: Alfred A. Knopf, 2005), 250-251, 264-265.

PAGE 19

Odin discovers runes:
- *Landscape and Memory*, 84-85.
- *The Poetic Edda*, trans. Lee M. Hollander (Austin: University of Texas Press, 1986), Hávamál, stanzas 138-163.

Puritans and beeches:
- *National Audubon Field Guide to North American Trees, Eastern Region*, 380-381.

Plains tribes and sacred trees:
- *The Earth Shall Weep*, 259.
- Thomas E. Mails, *Sundancing: The Great Sioux Piercing Ritual* (Tulsa: Council Oaks Books, 1978), 14, 37-138.

Glastonbury hawthorn:
- Luke Salkeld, "Were anti-Christians behind pilgrimage site attack? 2,000-year-old Holy Thorn Tree of Glastonbury is cut down," *Daily Mail*, December 9, 2010. Accessed April 22, 2018. http://www.dailymail.co.uk/news/article-1337159/Glastonburys-2000-year-old-Holy-Thorn-Tree-hacked-vandals.html.
- *Landscape and Memory*, 220-221.

hot and total ruin I sign my name here:
- *The Birth-mark*, 82.

PAGE 20

Green-Wood as useless ground:
• *Brooklyn's Green-Wood Cemetery*, 10.

Green-Wood named; the greenwood as a lawless realm:
• *Landscape and Memory*, 141.
• *Green-Wood: A History*, 14.

Douglass, sculptor of the cemetery:
• David Bates Douglass, *Exposition of the Plan and Objects of the Green-Wood Cemetery, an Incorporated Trust Chartered by the Legislature of the State of New York* (New York: Narine & Co., 1839, reprinted by Green-Wood Cemetery, Brooklyn, NY, 2006), 6, 11-12.

Douglass, surveyor of the Michigan Territory:
• Philip Heslip. "David Bates Douglass Biography." David Bates Douglass Papers 1812-1873. October 2009. Accessed April 22, 2018. https://quod.lib.umich.edu/c /clementsmss/umich-wcl-M-1390dou?view=text.
• Willis Frederick Dunbar, and George S. May, *Michigan: a history of the Wolverine State* (Grand Rapids, MI: Wm. B. Eerdmans Publishing Co., 1995), 158.

PAGE 21

Grave owners donate fences for bullets:
• *Brooklyn's Green-Wood Cemetery*, 21-23.

PAGE 22

Colonists' *unconquerable aversion to trees:*
• *Americans and their Forests*, 5, 55, 117, 120-128.
• Isaac Weld, *Travels Through the States of North America and the States of Upper and Lower Canada During the Years 1795, 1796, and 1797.* 2 vols., 2nd ed. (London: John Stockdale, 1799), 232, 41.

Salmon nutrients in trees:
• Marc Nelitz, et al., *Managing Pacific Salmon for Ecosystem Values: Ecosystem Indicators and the Wild Salmon Policy*, (Vancouver: Pacific Fisheries Resource Conservation Council, 2006), 13.
• *Last Stand of the Great Bear*, National Geographic Documentary, 2006. Accessed April 25, 2018. https://www.snagfilms.com/films/title/last_stand_of_the_great_bear.

Lore of the yew; yew as source of cancer drug:
• *Victorian Celebration of Death*, 41-42.
• "Science and Nature Team Up Against Breast and Ovarian Cancers." National Cancer Institute. March 31, 2015. Accessed April 22, 2018. https://www.cancer .gov/research/progress/discovery/taxol.

Chill/ Fingers of yew be curled/ Down on us:

- T.S. Eliot, "Burnt Norton," *Four Quartets* (San Diego: Harvest/HBJ, 1971), 18.

Emerson's pine tree poem:

- Emerson, "Woodnotes II," *The Complete Works of Ralph Waldo Emerson,* Vol. IX, *Poems.* Accessed April 22, 2018. http://www.rwe.org/category/rwe-org-complete-works-of-rwe/ix-poems/.

PAGE 23

Green-Wood incorporated:

- *Green-Wood: A History,* 9.
- *Exposition of the Plan and Objects of the Green-Wood Cemetery,* 3.

Emerson letter to Van Buren:

- Emerson, "Letter to President Van Buren." *The Complete Works of Ralph Waldo Emerson, Vol. III, Letters.* Accessed April 22, 2018. http://www.rwe.org/iii-letter-to-president-van-buren/.

Trail of Tears:

- *Mind on Fire,* 275-279.
- *The Earth Shall Weep,* 164-170.
- Stuart Banner, *How the Indians Lost Their Land: Law and Power on the Frontier* (Cambridge: The Belknap Press of Harvard University Press, 2005), 191.

Indians in New England a *picturesque antiquity*:

- *The Earth Shall Weep,* 44.
- *How the Indians Lost Their Land,* 153, 218.
- *The Ralph Waldo Emerson Journals, Vol. 7 1845-1848* (New York: Ralph Waldo Emerson Institute digital archive from the 1904-14 edition, ed. Edward Emerson, 2006), 19.

Emerson eulogy for Thoreau:

- Emerson. "Henry David Thoreau (Eulogy)." *The Complete Works of Ralph Waldo Emerson.* Accessed April 22, 2018. http://www.rwe.org/henry-david-thoreau-eulogy/.

Cherokee society:

- Duane Champagne, "Economic Culture, Institutional Order, and Sustained Market Enterprise: Comparisons of Historical and Contemporary American Indian Cases," in *Property Rights and Indian Economies,* Terry L. Anderson, ed. (Lanham, MD: Rowan & Littlefield Publishers, Inc., 1992), 198-99.
- Leonard A. Carlson, "Learning to Farm: Indian Land Tenure and Farming Before the Dawes Act," in *Property Rights and Indian Economies,* 70.

Emerson's dream of eating the world; *our days demand fire*:

- *The Mind on Fire,* 342, 572.

PAGE 25

Cleaveland, headmaster:

- Cleaveland, *A History of Bowdoin College, with biographical sketches of its graduates, from 1806 to 1879*, edited and completed by Alpheus Spring Packard (Boston: J.R. Osgood & Co., 1882), 172.

Cleaveland on gravesite etiquette:

- Cleaveland, *Hints Concerning Green-Wood, its Monuments and Improvements* (New York: Pudney & Russell, 1853), 41.

PAGE 26

Cleaveland on the Puritans:

- Cleaveland, *An Address Delivered at Topsfield in Massachusetts, August 28, 1850: the Two Hundredth Anniversary of the Incorporation of the Town* (New York: Pudney & Russell, 1851), 19, 44.
- Cleaveland, *An address delivered before the New-England Society of Brooklyn, N.Y., December 21, 1849* (New York: The Society, 1850), 20.

Puritan fear of becoming like Indians:

- John Canup, *Out of the Wilderness: the Emergence of an American Identity in Colonial New England* (Middletown, CT: Wesleyan University Press, 1990), 101-102, 149-197.
- Increase Mather, "An Earnest Exhortation To the Inhabitants of New-England," (Boston: John Foster, 1676).

Republic requires restraint:

- Ellen Paul Frankel and Howard Dickman, eds. *Liberty, Property, and the Foundations of the American Constitution*, (Albany: State University of New York Press, 1989), 6, 24-27,94, 131-132.
- Forrest McDonald, *Novus Ordo Seclorum: The Intellectual Origins of the Constitution* (Lawrence, KS: University Press of Kansas, 1985), 70-74.
- Gordon S. Wood, *The Creation of the American Republic 1776-1787* (Chapel Hill: University of North Carolina Press, 1998), 52-53, 66-69.

Second Inaugural Address of George W. Bush, January 20, 2005:

- George W. Bush, "Second Inaugural Address," Inaugural Addresses of the Presidents of the United States : From George Washington 1789 to George Bush 1989." Avalon Project - Documents in Law, History and Diplomacy, Yale University. 2008. Accessed April 22, 2018. http://avalon.law.yale.edu/21st_century/gbush2.asp.

Religion and profit *jump together*:

- Edward Winslow. *Good Newes from New England*, Introduction. 1624. "The Plymouth Colony Archive Project." December 14, 2007. Accessed April 22, 2018. http://www.histarch.illinois.edu/plymouth/goodnews0.html.
- Richard Pipes, *Property and Freedom* (New York: Alfred A. Knopf, 1999), 17.

Republican fear of luxury:
- *Creation of the American Republic*, 52.
- *Novus Ordo Seclorum*, 70-74.
- Ronald T. Takaki, *Iron Cages: Race and Culture in 19th-Century America* (Seattle: University of Washington Press, 1979), 4-11.

Cleaveland on need for restraint even in death:
- *Hints Concerning Green-Wood*, 39.

PAGE 28

juicy intervals; substances that travel across:
- Lisa Robertson, *Occasional Work and Seven Walks from the Office for Soft Architecture* (Astoria, Oregon: Clear Cut Press, 2003), 139-149.

PAGE 29

Relationship between Cleaveland and Emerson:
- *An Address Delivered at Topsfield*, 35-36.
- *The Mind on Fire*, "Genealogy."
- Cleaveland, *The First Century of Dummer Academy, A Historical Discourse Delivered at Newbury, Byfield Parish*, August 12, 1863 (Boston: Nichols & Noyes, 1865), 22-23.

Cleaveland on Green-Wood's gate:
- *A Hand-book*, 15-16.

Gothic architecture mimics trees:
- *Landscape and Memory*, 228-239.

Vitruvius, the best buildings echo the body:
- Bill Thayer. "Vitruvius: On Architecture." Lacus Curtius. Accessed April 22, 2018. http://penelope.uchicago.edu/Thayer/E/Roman/Texts/Vitruvius/home.html.

PAGE 30

Wood drove the nation's industrialization:
- *Americans and Their Forests*, 53-386.
- *Coal: A Human History*, 103-128, 137.

Emerson, "Address to the Inhabitants of Concord at the Consecration of Sleepy Hollow":
- Emerson, *Miscellanies* (Boston and New York: Houghton, Mifflin and Company, 1904), 431.

Infinite forest, infinite Indian labor:
- Silvia Federici, *Caliban and the Witch: Women, the Body and Primitive Accumulation* (Brooklyn: Autonomedia, 2004), 85.

Whitman's dream:
- Whitman, "Specimen Days," in *Whitman: Poetry and Prose* (New York: Literary Classics of the United States, Inc., 1996), 840.

PAGE 31

Cleaveland on the view from Ocean Hill:
- *A Hand-book*, 57.

PAGE 32

The logging continued unchecked:
- *Americans and Their Forests*, 353.

Joyce Kilmer, "Trees":
- "Trees." Poetry Foundation. Accessed April 22, 2018. https://www.poetry
  foundation.org/poetrymagazine/poems/12744/trees.

A consciousness about the forest:
- *Americans and Their Forests*, 16, 112, 144-145, 393-395.
- *Landscape and Memory*, 191-193.
- Henry Ward Beecher, "A Walk Among Trees," *Star Papers; or, Experiences of Art and Nature* (New York: J.B. Ford and Company, 1873), 272.

Cleaveland tree anxiety:
- *Green-Wood Cemetery: A History*, 137.
- *Hints Concerning Green-Wood*, 11-12.

PAGE 34

Raccoons:
- "Raccoon Videos, News and Facts." BBC Nature. Accessed April 22, 2018.
  http://www.bbc.co.uk/nature/life/Raccoon#p008wh5r.

Virginia Algonquian:
- John Noble Wilford, "Linguists Find The Words, And Pocahontas Speaks Again," *New York Times*, March 7, 2006.

PAGE 35

The first major engagement of the Revolution:
- *Green-Wood Cemetery: A History*, 11-12, 118-125.
- *Brooklyn's Green-Wood Cemetery*, 187-188.
- Edwin G. Burrows and Mike Wallace, *Gotham: A History of New York to 1898* (New York: Oxford University Press, 1999), 235-237.

Bones on the roof of Deutsche Bank:
- Kareem Fahim and Anthony DePalma, "9/11 Victims' Kin Assail Search for Remains," *New York Times*, July 15, 2006.
- Greg B. Smith, "Don't Bank on Anything. Search for remains stalls as safety clouds Deutsche's fate," *New York Daily News*, May 14, 2006.

Green-Wood fights for Battle Hill:
- *Green-Wood Cemetery: A History*, 13, 134-135.

Sale of Deutsche Bank building:
- Amy Westfeldt, "Tower with World Trade Center dust, human remains looms at ground zero," Associated Press, May 20, 2006.

Backup systems in Dublin keep world economy going:
- Sean O'Driscoll, "Dublin stepped in to run Deutsche on 9/11," *London Times*, June 4, 2006.

PAGE 38

Land ownership new to Puritans:
- *Property and Freedom*, 106, 126.
- *Novus Ordo Seclorum*, 11, 14.
- John Hanson Mitchell, *Trespassing: an inquiry into the private ownership of land* (Reading, MA: Addison-Wesley, 1998), 80-84.
- G.E. Mingay, *Parliamentary Enclosure in England: an Introduction to its Causes, Incidence, and Impact, 1750-1850*, (New York: Addison Wesley Longman, 1997), 11-14.
- J.M. Neeson, *Commoners: Common Right, Enclosure and Social Change in England, 1700-1820* (Cambridge: Cambridge University Press, 1993), 21.

Pilgrims and private plots:
- William Bradford. "Of Plymouth Plantation." Early Americas Digital Archive (EADA). Accessed April 22, 2018. http://eada.lib.umd.edu/text-entries/of-plymouth-plantation/.
- Bernard H. Siegan, *Property Rights from Magna Carta to the Fourteenth Amendment* (New Brunswick & London: Transaction Publishers, 2001), 55-56.

Property ownership as founding principle:
- *Novus Ordo Seclorum*, 74-75, 153.
- *Property and Freedom*, 113-114.

Private property in Green-Wood:
- *Exposition of the Plan and Objects of the Green-Wood Cemetery*, 4, 16-18.

Cleaveland's vexations and enthusiasms:
- *Hints Concerning Green-Wood*, 17, 41.
- Cleaveland, *Green-Wood: A Directory for Visitors* (New York: Pudney & Russell, 1857), 185.

PAGE 39

Tulip trees:
- "Specimen Days," 840.
- *National Audubon Society Field Guide to North American Trees, Eastern Region*, 436-437.

The word "forest" forms a fence:
- *Landscape and Memory*, 140-147.

- *Trespassing: An inquiry into the private ownership of land*, 82-83.
- *Parliamentary Enclosure*, 102-142.

Property rights as invisible fence, Jefferson's Land Ordinance:
- *Property Rights from Magna Carta to the Fourteenth Amendment*, 33.
- "Land Ordinance of 1785." Ohio History Central. Accessed April 22, 2018. http://www.ohiohistorycentral.org/w/Land_Ordinance_of_1785?rec=1472.

Native societies forced to contemplate a new reality:
- Ginette Aley, "Bringing About the Dawn: Agriculture, Internal Improvements, Indian Policy, and Euro-American Hegemony in the Old Northwest 1800-1846" in *The Boundaries Between Us: Natives and Newcomers Along the Frontiers Of the Old Northwest Territory, 1750-1850*, ed. Daniel P. Barr (Kent, Ohio: Kent State University Press, 2006), 201.
- "Learning to Farm: Indian Land Tenure and Farming Before the Dawes Act," in *Property Rights and Indian Economies*, 67-82.

PAGE 41

Give it no name:
- Roger Ebert, "Make it Green," *Chicago Sun-Times*, September 14, 2001.

World Trade Center site as meditative garden:
- Philip Nobel, *Sixteen Acres: Architecture and the Outrageous Struggle for the Future of Ground Zero* (New York: Metropolitan Books, 2005), 98-99.

"The tomb unfolding zero":
- Barbara Guest, "Egypt," *Selected Poems* (Los Angeles: Sun & Moon Press, 1995), 56-57.

World Trade Center as valuable real estate:
- *Sixteen Acres*, 1-2.
- Paul Goldberger, *Up from Zero, Politics, Architecture, and the Rebuilding of New York* (New York: Random House, 2004), 120-123.
- Deborah Sontag, "The Hole in the City's Heart," *New York Times*, September 11, 2006.

Emerson, inevitability of private property:
- *The Mind on Fire*, 401, 433-435.

Common fields as myth:
- Rachel Crawford, *Poetry, Enclosure, and the Vernacular Landscape 1700-1830* (Cambridge: Cambridge University Press, 2002), 56-62.

warre is a good tree:
- William C. Carroll, "The Nursery of Beggary," in *Enclosure Acts: Sexuality, Property, and Culture in Early Modern England* eds. Richard Burt and John Michael Archer (Ithaca, NY: Cornell University Press, 1994), 39.

PAGE 43

End of the forest, "lumber" as obstacle:
- *Coal: A Human History*, 104.
- *Americans and Their Forests*, 4, 13, 244-252, 432.

Franklin on "whites" and the forest:
- *Iron Cages*, 14.
- Benjamin Franklin. "Founders Online: Observations Concerning the Increase of Mankind, 1751." National Archives and Records Administration. Accessed April 22, 2018. https://founders.archives.gov/documents/Franklin/01-04-02-0080.

Cass on Indians disappearing with the forest:
- *Iron Cages*, 83.
- Lewis Cass, "Removal of the Indians," *North American Review*, Jan. 1830.

Forests like a blinding mist, like air:
- *Americans and their Forests*, 54-55, 81.
- Alexis de Tocqueville, *Democracy in America*, trans. Arthur Goldhammer (New York: Literary Classics of the United States, Inc., 2004), 25-26.

PAGE 44

Landscape gardening in America, and Emerson:
- A.J. Downing, *A Treatise on the Theory and Practice of Landscape Gardening, Adapted to North America* (New York: Riker, Thorne & Co., Sixth Edition, 1859), viii-x, 47.
- Elizabeth Barlow Rogers, *Landscape Design: A Cultural and Architectural History* (New York: Harry N. Abrams, Inc., 2001), 232-233, 325-330.
- *The Mind on Fire*, 433-435.

English gardens and Enclosure Acts:
- *Landscape Design*, 237-244.
- *Parliamentary Enclosure*, 124-125.

hunters, hoping their darling:
- Diane Ward, "Naming the Baby," in *Film-Yoked Scrim* (Queens, NY: Factory School Books, 2006), 21.

Plymouth and Concord, Indian villages:
- *1491*, 54-56.
- *The Earth Shall Weep*, 74-77.
- Emerson, "Historical Discourse at Concord." *The Complete Works of Ralph Waldo Emerson*. December 18, 2004. Accessed April 22, 2018. http://www.rwe.org/ii-historical-discourse-at-concord/.

What is the Earth itself:
- "Historical Discourse at Concord."

what is this separate nature?
- Whitman, "Passage to India," *Poetry and Prose*, 534.

PAGE 45

Emerson on snapping turtles:
- Emerson, "Courage," *The Complete Works of Ralph Waldo Emerson*. December 16, 2004. Accessed April 22, 2018. http://www.rwe.org/chapter-x-courage/.

PAGE 46

Private property at the heart of the Constitution:
- Jennifer Nedelsky, *Private Property and the Limits of American Constitutionalism* (Chicago: University of Chicago Press, 1990), 1-10.
- Michael Kamen, "The Rights of Property, and the Property in Rights, the Problematic Nature of 'Property' in the Political Thought of the Founders of the Early Republic," in *Liberty, Property and the Foundations of the American Constitution*, 1-11, 142.
- *Property Rights from Magna Carta to the Fourteenth Amendment*, 62.

Property as the "fence" to freedom:
- Edward J. Erler, "The Great Fence to Liberty: The Right to Property in the American Founding," in *Liberty, Property and the Foundations of the American Constitution*, 50-56.
- *Property Rights from Magna Carta to the Fourteenth Amendment*, 46-49.

On planting inedible fences:
- *Commoners: Common Right*, 29.

not flowers, but bone:
- James Trilling, *Ornament: A Modern Perspective* (Seattle: University of Washington Press, 2003), 223.

PAGE 48

Marines pull down Hussein statue:
- Ken Valenti, "Ground Zero War Rally," *The Journal News* (Westchester County, NY), April 11, 2003, 1A.
- Cameron McWhirter, "Special Report: The Road to Baghdad," *Atlanta Journal Constitution*, April 13, 2003.
- Michelle Maitre, "E. Bay Marine put noose on statue," *Alameda Times-Star*, April 11, 2003.

USS New York:
- "The USS New York, A Brief History." The US Navy. Accessed April 22, 2018. http://www.navy.mil/ussny/ny_history.asp

Steel from the towers in toasters:
- *Sixteen Acres*, 44.

Shays' Rebellion:
- *Novus Ordo Seclorum*, 176-179.
- *Private Property*, 30, 186.
- *Property Rights from Magna Carta to the Fourteenth Amendment*, 63-65.

Commoners compared to Indians:
- *Commoners: Common Right*, 30-31.

PAGE 49

Larry Silverstein:
- Deborah Sontag, "The Hole in the City's Heart," 3-5.
- Caitlin Kelly, "Who Is This Silverstein Guy? Real estate tycoon builds nothing but anger at WTC. Larry's Got To Go!" *New York Daily News*, April 23, 2006.

Leo Nedelsky:
- Nick Guroff, "Original Oppenheimer student dies at 102," *Santa Cruz Sentinel*, July 22, 2006.

Constitution protects unequal property:
- *Private Property*, 28-32.
- *Liberty, Property, and the Foundations of the American Constitution*, 10-11, 69

Freedom Tower on old Hudson River land:
- *Sixteen Acres*, 216-17.

The first sawmill; the British Navy commandeers American trees:
- *Americans and their Forests*, 90-92.
- *Novus Ordo Seclorum*, 32.

PAGE 50

Moses Cleaveland and the Western Reserve:
- "Cleaveland, Moses." Case Western Reserve University: Encyclopedia of Cleveland History. Accessed April 22, 2018. https://case.edu/ech/articles/c/cleaveland -moses/.
- William Ganson Rose, *Cleveland: the Making of a City* (Kent, Ohio: Kent State University Press, 1990), 22-25.

Paper money vs. land:
- *Novus Ordo Seclorum*, 94-95.
- *Creation of the American Republic*, 51.
- *Liberty, Property, and the Foundations of the American Constitution*, 94.
- *How the Indians Lost Their Land*, 100.

London as the greenwood:
- John L. McMullan, *The Canting Crew: London's Criminal Underworld 1550-1700*, (New Brunswick, NJ: Rutgers University Press, 1984), 15.

- Maurizio Gotti, *The Language of Thieves and Vagabonds: 17th and 18th Century Canting Lexicography in England* (Tubingen: Max Niemeyer Verlag, 1999), 5-17.

PAGE 52

DeWitt Clinton, Douglass and the Erie Canal:
- Gerard T. Koeppel, *Water for Gotham: A History* (Princeton: Princeton University Press, 2001), 158.
- Pranay Gupte, "Remaking a Cemetery Into a Cultural Treasure," *New York Sun*, September 1, 2005.

Cleaveland on Indians; natives imbued with ghostliness:
- *A Hand-book*, 23.
- *The Earth Shall Weep*, xxii.

Moses Cleaveland and the founding of Cleveland:
- "Cleaveland, Moses." Case Western Reserve University: Encyclopedia of Cleveland History.
- R. Douglas Hurt, *The Ohio Frontier: Crucible of the Old Northwest, 1720-1830* (Bloomington: Indiana University Press, 1996), 199.

Destruction of Ohio's forests; Cuyahoga catches on fire:
- *Americans and Their Forests*, 361-368.
- *Cleveland: the Making of a City*, 32.
- The Cuyahoga River Online Exhibition. Accessed April 22, 2018. http://www.clevelandmemory.org/speccoll/croe/index.html.

PAGE 53

Stephen Charles Vincent:
- Edward Wong and Fakr al-Haider, "U.S. Journalist Who Wrote About Police Corruption Is Abducted and Killed in Basra," *New York Times*, August 4, 2005.
- Robert F. Worth, Ali Adeeb, Abdul Razzaq al-Saiedy, and Qais Mizher, "Reporter Working for Times Abducted and Slain in Iraq," *New York Times*, September 20, 2005.
- Kirk Semple, "Reporter's Death Reflects the Dread of a City Filled With Rumors and Violence," *New York Times*, October 9, 2005.

PAGE 54

Andrew Jackson Downing:
- "Andrew Jackson Downing," Encyclopædia Britannica. May 9, 2018. Accessed May 28, 2018. https://www.britannica.com/biography/Andrew-Jackson-Downing.
- "Andrew Jackson Downing," FrederickLawOlmsted.com. Accessed April 22, 2018. http://www.fredericklawolmsted.com/ajdowning.htm.

Downing on trees:
- *A Treatise on the Theory and Practice of Landscape Gardening*, 69-274, see especially 69-70 and 103-104.

World Trade Center Memorial:
- "Build the Memorial First," *The New York Times*, March 10, 2006.
- *Up from Zero*, 227.

Douglass followed Downing's principles:
- *A Hand-book*, 13-14.
- *Hints Concerning Green-Wood*, 3.

Indian ecology destroyed by colonists:
- Andrew Delbanco, *The Puritan Ordeal* (Cambridge, MA: Harvard University Press, 1989), 94.
- *1491*, 264, 315-323.
- *Out of the Wilderness*, 25-26.

PAGE 57-58

Downing on American gardening:
- *A Treatise on the Theory and Practice of Landscape Gardening*, vii-ix, 19-23.

Dawes Act:
- *The Earth Shall Weep*, 303-305.
- *Iron Cages*, 188-193.
- *How the Indians Lost Their Land*, 260.

Chief Bushyhead:
- *How the Indians Lost Their Land*, 264.

Beecher and his elm:
- "A Walk Among the Trees," *Star Papers*, 279-280.
- Debby Applegate, *The Most Famous Man in America: The Biography of Henry Ward Beecher* (New York: Doubleday, 2006), 269-271.

The Dream of the Rood:
- "Dream of the Rood," AngloSaxon Narrative Poetry Project. Accessed April 22, 2018. https://anglosaxonpoetry.camden.rutgers.edu/dream-of-the-rood/.
- *Landscape and Memory*, 219.

PAGE 60

Family names from the forest:
- William Bryant Logan, *Oak, the Frame of Civilization* (New York: W.W. Norton & Co. Inc., 2005), 22-23.

World Trade Center Memorial grove:
- "WTC Memorial Foundation Selects New York Capital Region Trees To Be Part of WTC Memorial." Accessed, May 14, 2007. http://www.national911memorial.org.

122

van Gogh on pollard willows:
- Jonathan Jones, "This land is our land: Gainsborough, Constable, Turner . . . a few great painters have shaped the way we see the countryside," *The Guardian*, June 28, 2001.

Emerson on shipwreck:
- *The Ralph Waldo Emerson Journals, Vol. III 1833-1835*, 82.

PAGE 61

Bloomberg says "Suck it up":
- "The Hole in the City's Heart," 13.

Cleaveland autobiography:
- *A History of Bowdoin College*, 173.
- *Hints Concerning Green-Wood*, 44.

Emerson on self control:
- Emerson, "Letters and Social Aims." *The Complete Works of Ralph Waldo Emerson, Vol. III.* January 23, 2005. Accessed April 22, 2018. http://www.rwe.org/vol-viii -letters-and-social-aims/.

Giuliani says go shopping:
- Deroy Murdock, "Giuliani's Finest Hour," *The National Review*, September 14, 2001.
- Fred Kaplan, "In crisis, Giuliani's image transformed," *Boston Globe*, September 14, 2001.

PAGE 63

Oliver Goldsmith, "The Deserted Village":
- "The Deserted Village," Accessed April 22, 2018. http://web.archive.org/ web/20080512013120/.
- *A History of the Conception of Death*, 347.
- *Parliamentary Enclosure*, 124-125.

Images of "Indian freedom":
- *1491*, 329-337.

Property as myth:
- *Private Property*, 8-9, 222-240, 259-260.

Remains at World Trade Center site:
- Michael Daly, "His Prophecy from the Pit Comes True," *New York Daily News*, October 22, 2006.
- Peter Kadushin and Paul II.B. Shin, "15 More Remains Recovered at WTC," *New York Daily News*, October 22, 2006.
- David W. Dunlap, "Ground Zero Forensic Team Is Posted to Seek Remains," *New York Times*, October 21, 2006, B2.

Public protests plans for WTC site:

- Georgett Roberts and Maggie Haberman, "It's Thumbs Down: Planners Backpedal After Hundreds Pan WTC Designs," *New York Post*, July 21, 2002.
- Edward Wyatt and Charles V. Bagli, "Visions of Ground Zero: The Public; Officials Rethink Building Proposal for Ground Zero," *New York Times*, July 21, 2002.

Plans respect private property rights:

- *Up from Zero*, 100.

The "ha-ha":

- *Landscape and Memory*, 539.
- *Landscape Design*, 238.

PAGE 64

Granite

- Colin Tudge, *The Tree: a Natural History of What Trees Are, How They Live, and Why They Matter* (New York: Three Rivers Press, 2005), 284.
- "Granite." World of Earth Science. 2018. Accessed April 22, 2018. https://www .encyclopedia.com/earth-and-environment/geology-and-oceanography/geology -and-oceanography/granite.

Cleaveland on granite:

- *Hints Concerning Green-Wood*, 35.

PAGE 66

the vanished/ dress us in skin:

- Alicia Cohen, "Vertigo," *Debts and Obligations* (Oakland: O Books, 2008), 23.

Green-Wood's parrots:

- "Brooklyn Parrots," BrooklynParrotscom. Accessed April 22, 2018. http:// brooklynparrots.com/.
- "Go Birding, Green-Wood Cemetery." New York City Audubon Society. Accessed April 22, 2018. http://www.nycaudubon.org/brooklyn-birding/green-wood-cemetery.

PAGE 67-68

The Flowers Personified

- J.J. Grandville, Taxile DeLord, and Alphonse Carr, *The Flowers Personified*, trans. Nehemiah Cleaveland (New York: R. Martin, 1859).

the in, in, in:

- Katerina Anghelaki-Rooke, "My Mother and Satan," in Gail Holst-Warhaft, *Dangerous Voices: Women's Laments and Greek Literature* (London: Routledge, 1995), 186.

Green-Wood's use of herbicides:

- Phone conversation with Tom Cush of Earth Care Lawn and Tree, 2006.

Effects of pendimethalin and 2,4-D:

- "Pendimethalin." Extonet. September 93. Accessed April 22, 2018. http://pmep .cce.cornell.edu/profiles/extoxnet/metiram-propoxur/pendimethalin-ext.html.

- "Pendimethalin." National Center for Biotechnology Information. PubChem Compound Database. Accessed April 22, 2018. https://pubchem.ncbi.nlm.nih .gov/compound/pendimethalin#section=Safety-and-Hazards.

Ladies' botanies:

- Caroline Jackson-Houlston, "'Queen Lilies'? The Interpenetration of Scientific, Religious and Gender Discourses in Victorian Representations of Plants," *Journal of Victorian Culture*, Vol. 11, No. 1 (Spring 2006), 87-96.
- Vera Norwood, *Made from this Earth: American Women and Nature* (Chapel Hill: University of North Carolina Press, 1993), 12.

PAGE 69

George Arents:

- Martin Hunter, "A Universe of Tobacciana - The George Arents Collection." *Pipes Magazine*. 1998. Accessed April 22, 2018. http://pipesmagazine.com/blog /pipesmoke/a-universe-of-tobacciana-the-george-arents-collection/.
- Nicholas A. Basbanes, *A Gentle Madness: Bibliophiles, Bibliomanes, and the Eternal Passion for Books* (New York: Macmillan, 1999), 356.

PAGE 70

The study of botany could be dangerous for ladies:

- "Queen Lilies," 86.
- Paul Lawrence Farber, *Finding Order in Nature: The Naturalist Tradition from Linnaeus to E. O. Wilson* (Baltimore: The Johns Hopkins University Press, 2000), 9.
- Alphonse Karr, *The Ladies' Botany in The Flowers Personified* trans. Nehemiah Cleaveland (New York: R. Martin, 1859), i, 15.

On hysteria:

- Tina Darragh, "Illuminated Apology Lament: Precautionary Hysteria," *opposable dumbs* (Greenbelt, MD: self published, 2007), unpaginated.

PAGE 71

Professional mourners:

- *Dangerous Voices: Women's Laments and Greek Literature*, 1-6.
- Richard A. Hughes, *Lament, Death, and Destiny* (New York: Peter Lang, 2004), 2-3, 18.

Flora caused the birth of Mars:

- Ovid, *Fasti*, trans. James George Frazer (Cambridge, MA: Harvard University Press, 1931), 279.

Repression of lament:

- *Lament, Death and Destiny*, 14-23.
- *opposable dumbs*, unpaginated.

PAGE 73

J.J. Grandville:
- Peter A. Wick, *The Court of Flora* (New York: George Braziller, 1981), unpag. introduction.
- Clive F. Getty, "Grandville: Opposition Caricature and Political Harassment," *Print Collector's Newsletter* Vol. XIV, No. 6 (Jan-Feb. 1984), 197-201.
- J.J. Grandville, *Public and Private Life of Animals*, intro. by Edward Lucie-Smith (London: Paddington Press, 1977), vi.

Repression during the July Monarchy:
- Judith Wechsler, *A Human Comedy: Physiognomy and Caricature in 19th Century Paris* (Chicago: The University of Chicago Press, 1982), 71.
- Elise K. Kenney and John M. Merriman, *The Pear: French Graphic Arts in the Golden Age of Caricature* (South Hadley, MA: Mt. Holyoke College Art Museum), 20.

Plato bans poetry:
- *Lament, Death, Destiny*, 160.
- Plato, "The Republic." The Internet Classics Archive. Accessed April 22, 2018. http://classics.mit.edu/Plato/republic.11.x.html.

Vesalius and human dissection:
- Harold J. Morowitz, *Entropy and the Magic Flute* (Oxford: Oxford University Press, 1993) 37-39.
- *Caliban and the Witch*, 132, 157, note 13.

PAGE 74

Monsters begin to appear:
- Hank Steuver, "Summer's Bumper Crop of Monsters," *The Washington Post*, August 19, 2008. Accessed April 22, 2018. http://www.washingtonpost.com/wp-dyn/content/ article/2008/08/18/AR2008081802481.html?hpid=topnews.
- Richard Lawson, "Our Monsteriest Season Yet," *Gawker*, August 19, 2008. Accessed April 22, 2018. http://gawker.com/5038962/summer-2008--our-monsteriest-season-yet.

Emerson at the Cabinet of Natural History:
- David R Godine, "Transparency in the *Jardin des Plantes*," American Language Association, May, 2007, Boston. Accessed April 25, 2018. http://www.rwe.org/transparency-in-the-jardin-des-plantes/
- *The Mind on Fire*, 138-142.
- *The Ralph Waldo Emerson Journals*, Vol. III, digital collection prepared by Ralph Waldo Emerson Institute (2006), 161-162.

Grandville at the Cabinet; fear of arrest:
- "Opposition Caricature and Political Harassment," 200.

- *The Pear: French Graphic Arts in the Golden Age of Caricature* (South Hadley, MA: Mt. Holyoke College Art Museum), 108.

Kaluli believe the dead turn into flying things:
- Steven Feld, *Sound and Sentiment: Birds, Weeping, Poetics, and Song in Kaluli Expression*, Second Edition (Philadelphia: University of Pennsylvania Press, 1982), 53-56, 68.

Gabriello Fallopio:
- "Gabriel Fallopius," Encyclopædia Britannica. May 04, 1999. Accessed April 22, 2018. https://www.britannica.com/biography/Gabriel-Fallopius.
- "Gabriello Fallopio," Catholic Encyclopedia. Accessed April 22, 2018. http://www.newadvent.org/cathen/05772a.htm.

Emerson's wife fades from his journals:
- Lee Rust Brown, *The Emerson Museum: Practical Romanticism and the Pursuit of the Whole* (Cambridge, MA: Harvard University Press, 1997), 11.

PAGE 75

Cabinet exudes commerce and empire:
- *The Emerson Museum*, 79.
- *Finding Order in Nature*, 12.

French censors outlaw pears:
- *A Human Comedy*, 66-81, 100.

Church fathers adopt Plato's ban on lament:
- *Lament, Death, and Destiny*, 73-78.

looking back for anything/not burning:
- kari edwards, bharat jiva (Brooklyn: Venn Diagram Productions, 2009), 81.

hard light, clear edges:
- University of Illinois, "On Lowell, Pound, and Imagism." Accessed April 23, 2018. http://www.english.illinois.edu/maps/poets/g_l/amylowell/imagism.htm.

Obama relaxes ban on photos of coffins:
- "Pentagon to allow photos of soldiers' coffins," *New York Times*, February 26, 2009.
- "US lifts ban on war dead photos," BBC News, February 26, 2009.

PAGE 77

Green-Wood imports birds:
- *Green-Wood: A History*, 73, 134.

Kaluli women turn into birds; laments impregnated:
- *Sound and Sentiment*, 33-43, 92, 132.

127

St. Augustine on the death of his mother:
- *Lament, Death, and Destiny*, 77.
- "The Confessions and Letters of St. Augustine, with a Sketch of His Life and Work," Christian Classics Ethereal Library. Accessed April 23, 2018. http://www.ccel.org/ccel/schaff/npnf101.vi.IX.XII.html.

Grandville's animals rise up:
- *A Human Comedy*, 100-101.

Ovid's battle between order and chaos:
- Barbara Weidon Boyd, "Celabitur Auctor: The crisis of authority and narrative patterning in Ovid Fasti 5," *Phoenix*, Vol. 54, No. 1/2 (Spring-Summer 2000), 65, 95.

Link between women and flowers:
- *Ladies' Horticulture* in *The Flowers Personified*, 85.
- *Ladies' Botany*, 16.

Flora makes Juno pregnant:
- *Fasti*, 279.

I am the no and the yes:
- 'Annah Sobelman, "I Am the No and the Yes," *The Tulip Sacrament* (Hanover, NH: University Press of New England, 1995), 8.

Papua New Guinea:
- "Papua New Guinea." U.S. Department of State. February 07, 2017. Accessed April 23, 2018. https://www.state.gov/r/pa/ei/bgn/2797.htm.
- Ingrid Gascoigne, *Papua New Guinea* (Tarrytown, New York: Marshall Cavendish, 1998), 9, 26.

Birds of paradise:
- Pamela Swadling, *Plumes from paradise: trade cycles in outer Southeast Asia and their impact on New Guinea and nearby islands until 1920* (Boroko, Papua New Guinea: Papua New Guinea National Museum, 1996), 17, 49.
- Gordon Ramel, "The Birds of Paradise," The Earthlife Web. Accessed April 23, 2018. https://www.earthlife.net/birds/paradisidae.html.

New Guinea economy:
- "The World Factbook: Papua New Guinea." U.S. Central Intelligence Agency. April 03, 2018. Accessed April 23, 2018. https://www.cia.gov/library/publications/the-world-factbook/geos/pp.html.
- *Plumes from Paradise*, 17, 49.

Flora protects the commons; acorns:
- *Fasti*, 219, 280-281.

Give me the eye to see a navy in an acorn:
- *The Ralph Waldo Emerson Journals*, Vol. III, 290.

PAGE 80

Paris and political turmoil:
- *Emerson Museum*, 63-65.
- *Mind on Fire*, 138.
- Johannes Willms, *Paris, Capital of Europe: from the Revolution to the Belle Epoque* trans. Eveline L. Kanes (New York: Holmes & Meier, 1997), 233.

Classification system at Cabinet of Natural History:
- *The Ralph Waldo Emerson Journals*, Vol. III, 163.
- *Mind on Fire*, 138-142.
- *Emerson Museum*, 59-62.

Goethe and the ur-plant:
- Johann Wolfgang von Goethe, "The Metamorphosis of Plants." *Goethe's Collected Works*, Vol. 12, Scientific Studies (Princeton: Princeton University Press, 1994), 76-97.
- Alan P. Cotrell, "The Resurrection of Thinking and the Redemption of Faust: Goethe's New Scientific Attitude," in *Goethe's Way of Science: A Phenomenology of Nature*, eds. David Seamon and Arthur Zajonc (Albany: State University of New York Press, 1998), 260.
- Agnes Arbor, "Goethe's Botany," *Chronica Botanica*, Vol. 10, No. 2 (Summer, 1946), 81.

Emerson returns home:
- *Mind on Fire*, 138-181.
- *The Ralph Waldo Emerson Journals*, Vol. III, 156-171, 288.
- Emerson, "Representative Men," *The Complete Works of Ralph Waldo Emerson*. Accessed April 23, 2018. http://www.rwe.org/category/rwe-org-complete-works-of-rwe/iv-representative-men/.

Drawing speaks to the eyes:
- *A Human Comedy*, 81.

Agent Orange:
- Daniel Zwerdling, "The Legacy of Agent Orange," American Public Media. Accessed 23 April, 2018. http://americanradioworks.publicradio.org/features/vietnam/vnation/legacy.html
- William Glaberson, "Agent Orange, the Next Generation," *The New York Times*, August 8, 2004.
- Jacob Silverman, "How Agent Orange Worked." HowStuffWorks.com. November 4, 2008. Accessed April 23, 2018 https://science.howstuffworks.com/agent-orange.htm

PAGE 82

Link between gardening and motherhood:

- *Ladies' Horticulture*, 98.

The first bird of paradise skins:

- *Plumes from Paradise*, 64, 15.5.
- Robin W. Doughty, *Feather Fashions and Bird Preservation: A Study in Nature Protection* (Berkeley: University of California Press, 1975), 9-10.
- Alfred Russel Wallace, *The Malay Archipelago* (Singapore: Periplus Editions, 2002 [orig. 1846]), 419.

Green-Wood as nursery:

- *Brooklyn's Green-Wood Cemetery*, 102.
- Theodore Cuyler, *The empty crib* (London: R.D. Dickinson, 1872), 152.

Victorian infant mortality:

- Richard A. Meckel, *Save the Babies: American Public Health Reform and the Prevention of Infant Mortality*, 1850-1929 (Baltimore: The Johns Hopkins University Press, 1990), 11-42.
- Samuel H. Preston and Michael R. Haines, *Fatal Years: Child Mortality in Late Nineteenth-Century America* (Princeton: Princeton University Press, 1991), 1.
- Jeffrey Brosco, "The Early History of the Infant Mortality Rate in America: A Reflection Upon the Past and a Prophecy of the Future," *Pediatrics*, Vol. 103, No. 2, February 1999, 478-485.

Gimi believe male children come from birds:

- Paige West, *Conservation is Our Government Now: The Politics of Ecology in Papua New Guinea* (Durham, NC: Duke University Press, 2006), 83-87.

I was always dead, weren't you?:

- Alice Notley, "Lizard," *Desamere* (Berkeley: O Books, 1995), 129.

PAGE 83

Industrial revolution in Paris:

- Colin Jones, *Paris, the Biography of a City* (New York: Viking, 2005) 282-283, 296.
- Andrew Lees and Lynn Hollen Lees, *Cities and the Making of Modern Europe, 1750-1914* (Cambridge: Cambridge University Press, 2007), 288.

Paris like the New World:

- Honoré de Balzac, *Old Goriot*, trans. M.A. Crawford (London: Penguin, 1951), 133.
- Walter Benjamin, "The Paris of the Second Empire in Baudelaire," *Selected Writings*, Vol. 4 1938-1940 (Cambridge, MA: Harvard University Press, 2003), 22

Descriptions of the New Guinea jungle:

- Edward L. Schieffelin and Robert Crittenden, eds. *Like People You See in a Dream: First Contact in Six Papuan Societies* (Stanford: Stanford University Press, 1991), 58.

- *Conservation Is Our Government Now*, 2.
- *The Malay Archipelago*, 376.

Feather fashions:
- *Plumes from Paradise*, 83.
- *Feather Fashions and Bird Preservation*, 1-2, 17.

Benjamin on fashion:
- Walter Benjamin, *The Arcades Project*, trans. Howard Eiland and Kevin McLaughlin (Cambridge, MA: The Belknap Press of Harvard University Press, 1999) 8.

PAGE 84-85

Encounters with the bird of paradise:
- *Plumes from Paradise*, 73.

the useless a fire:
- Graham Foust, "Blood Test," *Necessary Stranger* (Chicago: Flood Editions, 2007), 41.

Goethe's pregnant point; and light:
- Arthur Zajonc, "Goethe and the Science of His Time," in *Goethe's Way of Science*, 27.
- "The Resurrection of Thinking and the Redemption of Faust," in *Goethe's Way of Science*, 267.
- Johann Wolfgang von Goethe, "Significant Help Given by an Ingenious Turn of Phrase," *Scientific Studies* trans. Douglas Miller (Princeton: Princeton University Press, 1994), 41; see also the Introduction for the controversy with Linnaeus.

Nature sodden with metaphor:
- Neil Smith, *Uneven Development: Nature, Capital, and the Production of Space* (Athens, GA: University of Georgia Press, 1990), 26.

the animal becomes its own language:
- Henri Bortoft, *The Wholeness of Nature: Goethe's Way Toward a Science of Conscious Participation in Nature* (Hudson, NY: Lindisfarne Books, 1996), 26.

there . . . arose a hunger to fix meaning:
- *A Human Comedy*, 8.
- "The Paris of the Second Empire in Baudelaire," 18-22.
- *Paris, Biography of a City*, 278, 296.
- *Emerson Museum*, 140.

Gimi attitudes toward the forest:
- *Conservation is our Government Now*, 79-81.

Cabinet of Natural history collects all life forms; depends on violence:
- *Finding Order*, 29-30. 37-42.
- Toby A. Appel, *The Cuvier-Geoffroy Debate: French Biology in the Decades before Darwin* (Oxford: Oxford University Press, 1987), 7. 17-18.

- Dorinda Outram, "New spaces in natural history," in *Cultures of Natural History*, eds. N. Jardine, J.A. Secord and E.C. Spary (Cambridge: Cambridge University Press, 1996), 249-258.
- Dorinda Outram, *Georges Cuvier: Vocation, Science and Authority in Post-Revolutionary France* (Manchester: Manchester University Press, 1984), 162-165.
- *Emerson Museum*, 131.
- Charles Coulston Gillispie, *Science and Polity in France: The Revolutionary and Napoleonic Years* (Princeton: Princeton University Press, 2004), 433-444.

Vietnam's DMZ as wildlife preserve:
- Eleanor Jane Sterling, Martha Maud Hurley, Le Duc Minh, *Vietnam: a Natural History* (New Haven: Yale University Press, 2006), 10-16, 42-43.
- Mary C. Pearl "Natural Selections: Roaming Free in the DMZ," *Discover* magazine, 11 November, 2006.

Wallace shoots orangutans:
- *The Malay Archipelago*, 28-49.
- Peter Raby, *Alfred Russel Wallace: A Life* (Princeton: Princeton University Press, 2001), 107-108.

PAGE 88-89

Nineteenth-century city as deadly:
- *Save the Babies*, 11-13.
- *Gotham: A History of New York City to 1898*, 361-62, 443, 576, 587-602.
- Howard P. Chudacoff, Judith E. Smith. *The Evolution of American Urban Society* (Upper Saddle River, NJ: Prentice Hall 2000), 17, 39-75.

How soon one feels as if one is suffocating:
- *Paris, Capital of Europe: from the Revolution to the Belle Epoque*, 215.

Realist novelists adopt methods of naturalists:
- *Emerson Museum*, 140.

Displays didn't resemble original animal; Wallace felt this loss:
- Anne Larsen, "Equipment for the Field" in *Cultures of Natural History*, 358-359.
- *The Malay Archipelago*, 326.
- *Alfred Russel Wallace: A Life*, 120.

New Yorkers wary of Green-Wood:
- *Green-Wood: A History*, 26-30, 52.

PAGE 90

Kaluli use metaphors of water:
- *Sound and Sentiment*, 163-170.

St. Gregory of Nyssa:
- Virginia Burrus, "Begotten Not Made": *Conceiving Manhood in Late Antiquity* (Stanford: Stanford University Press, 2000), 85-97, 120-121.

- Gregory of Nyssa, "On Virginity." Church Fathers. Accessed April 23, 2018. http://www.newadvent.org/fathers/2907.htm.
- *Lament, Death, and Destiny*, 74-75.

Green-Wood's lakes:

- *Green-Wood: A History*, 68.

Kaluli funeral rituals:

- *Sound and Sentiment*, 96.

PAGE 91

Naturalists compete for specimens:

- *Plumes from Paradise*, 73-74.
- *Conservation Is Our Government Now*, 2.
- *Finding Order*, 24.
- Gillian Beer, "Traveling the Other Way" in *Cultures of Natural History*, 325.

Method of hunting birds of paradise:

- *Plumes from Paradise*, 182.

The vogue for natural history:

- *Emerson Museum*, 60, 130-138.
- *Finding Order*, 30.
- *Georges Cuvier*, 181.

Grandville's *Un Autre Monde*:

- *A Human Comedy*, 101.
- *Arcades Project*, 885.
- Grandville, *Un Autre Monde* (Paris: H. Fournier, 1844).

Benjamin calls Grandville *the tribal sorcerer*:

- *Arcades Project*, 7, 186.

Emerson at Sleepy Hollow:

- Emerson, *Miscellanies* (Boston and New York: Houghton, Mifflin and Company, 1904), 434.

PAGE 92

Wallace fails to find birds of paradise:

- *Conservation Is Our Government Now*, 2-3.
- *The Malay Archipelago*, 381-389.
- Alfred Russel Wallace, *My Life: A Record of Events and Opinions*, Vol. 1 (New York: Dodd, Mead & Company, 1905), 389-394.

Wildlife markets in Vietnam:

- *Vietnam: A Natural History*, 318-329.

Arsenic to preserve animal skins:
- "Equipment for the Field," 370-372.
- William R. Cullen, *Is Arsenic an Aphrodisiac? The Sociochemistry of an Element* (London: The Royal Society of Chemistry, 2008), 82-83.

St. Ambrose on the death of his brother:
- St. Ambrose, "On the Death of Satyrus (Book II)." Church Fathers. Accessed April 23, 2018. http://www.newadvent.org/fathers/34032.htm.

Apes associated with satyrs:
- Jennifer Mason, *Civilized Creatures: Urban Animals, Sentimental Culture, and American Literature*, 1850–1900 (Baltimore: Johns Hopkins University Press, 2005), 79-80.
- Raymond Corbey, *The Metaphysics of Apes: Negotiating the Animal-Human Boundary* (Cambridge: Cambridge University Press, 2005), 38-45.

Satyrus and her twins:
- Medieval Bestiary: Ape. Accessed April 23, 2018. http://www.bestiary.ca/beasts /beast148.htm.
- Terence Hanbury White, Kenneth Frazier, *The book of beasts: being a translation from a Latin bestiary of the twelfth century* (Madison: The University of Wisconsin Madison Libraries Parallel Press, 1960), 34-36.

PAGE 93

Wallace on Waigeo; collected 125,000 specimens in his travels:
- *The Malay Archipelago*, 44, 121-122, 406.

The process of preserving birds:
- "Equipment for the Field," 371-372.

Orangutan in Malay; Linnaeus controversy:
- *The Metaphysics of Apes*, 39, 46-49.
- Georges Louis Leclerc Buffon, "The Nomenclature of the Apes," in *Buffon's Natural history: containing a theory of the earth, a general history of man, of the brute creation, and of vegetables, minerals, &c.* Vol. IX (London: J.S. Barr, 1792), 107-170.

PAGE 94

Botany did not require killing:
- Elizabeth B. Keeney, *The Botanizers: Amateur Scientists in Nineteenth-Century America* (Chapel Hill: The University of North Carolina Press, 1992), 43.

A young scientist came to save orangutans:
- Biruté M.F. Galdikas, *Reflections of Eden: My Years with the Orangutans of Borneo* (Boston: Little, Brown and Co. 1995), 212.

PAGE 95

Victorians found many uses for arsenic:
- *Is Arsenic an Aphrodisiac?* 19, 43, 99-115.
- Ian Burney, *Poison, Detection, and the Victorian Imagination* (Manchester: Manchester University Press, 2006), 64-66.

Grandville's death:
- *The Court of Flora*, unpag. intro.

Garden cemeteries as resorts; Whitman in Green-Wood:
- *Brooklyn's Green-Wood Cemetery*, 3-20.
- *The Collected Writings of Walt Whitman, The Journalism*, Vol. 1, 190-191.

Galdikas recalls an idyllic afternoon:
- *Reflections of Eden*, 203.

Galdikas on the cover of National Geographic:
- *Reflections of Eden*, photo plate after p. 120.
- Donna Haraway, *Primate Visions: Gender, Race, and Nature in the World of Modern Science* (New York: Routledge, 1989), 148.

PAGE 96

Benjamin's little hunchback:
- Walter Benjamin, *A Berlin Childhood around 1900,* trans. Howard Eiland (Cambridge, MA: The Belknap Press of Harvard University Press, 2006), 120-122.
- Walter Benjamin, *Illuminations: Essays and Reflections*, intro. by Hannah Arendt (New York: Harcourt Brace Jovanovich, Inc. 1968), 6-7.

Grandville's "Venus at the Opera":
- *A Human Comedy*, 102.
- *Un Autre Monde.*

Emerson on Goethe:
- Emerson, "Goethe; or, the Writer," 752.

Goethe's influence on Emerson and Benjamin:
- Rolf Tiedemann, "Dialectics at a Standstill: Approaches to the Passagen-Werk," *Arcades Project*, 931.
- David Harvey, *Paris, Capital of Modernity* (New York; Routledge, 2006) 18.
- *Illuminations*, Arendt intro, 12-14.
- *Goethe's Botany*, Agnes Arber intro., 80.

Benjamin and Emerson use techniques of natural history:
- Susan Buck-Morss, *The Dialectics of Seeing: Walter Benjamin and the Arcades Project* (Cambridge, MA: MIT Press, 1989), 59-74.
- *Emerson Museum*, 79-80.

Anxiety about arsenic poisonings:
- *Is Arsenic an Aphrodisiac?* 112-113.
- *Poison, Detection, and the Victorian Imagination*, 20-30.

New Guinea forest disappearing:
- Andrew C. Revkin, "Forest Disappearing in Papua New Guinea," *New York Times*, June 3, 2008.
- Michael Perry, "Satellite Images Reveal Papua Forest Destruction," Reuters, June 2, 2008.

PAGE 97

Grandville and Benjamin driven to death by Paris:
- *Arcades Project*, 7.
- *Illuminations*, 7.

Balzac compared Paris to a vast ocean:
- *Old Goriot*, 37-38.
- *Paris, Capital of Modernity*, 93.

Benjamin's poem:
- Momme Brodersen, *Walter Benjamin: A Biography*, trans. Malcom R. Green and Ingrida Ligers, ed. Martina Dervis (New York: Verso, 1996), 201.

Sugito's murders; Gundul's attack:
- *Reflections of Eden*, 293-295, 379, photo plate after 280.

PAGE 98

U.S. used arsenic in Vietnam; banned in U.S. as a pesticide:
- *Is Arsenic an Aphrodisiac?* 75-76, 257-258.
- Deborah Blum, "A is for Arsenic (Pesticides, if You Please)," *Wired*, June 19, 2012. Accessed 23 April, 2018. https://www.wired.com/2012/06/arsenic-pesticides-in
-our-food/

The Mekong River's many names:
- *Vietnam: A Natural History*, 266-270.

Wallace tried to keep animals alive:
- *Alfred Russel Wallace: A Life*, 80.
- Alfred Russel Wallace, *Infinite Tropics: an Alfred Russel Wallace Anthology*, ed. Andrew Berry (London: Verso, 2003), 294.

PAGE 99

Mass production alienated Grandville; flowers in haute couture:
- *Court of Flora*, unpag. intro.

Arsenic-treated wood:
- *Is Arsenic an Aphrodisiac?* 68.

American grass:
- *Vietnam: A Natural History*, 41-42.
- "The Legacy of Agent Orange," American Public Media.

French women echoed plants; fixation on feathers:
- Peter Wollen, "The Concept of fashion in the Arcades Project," in *Boundary 2, an international journal of literature and culture*, Vol. 30, No. 1 Spring 2003 (Durham, NC: Duke University Press), 136.
- *Feather Fashions*, 16.
- *Plumes from Paradise*, 84-85.

Women as the *four-footed companion of the man*:
- *The Arcades Project*, 80-81.

PAGE 100

Wallace obsessed with living birds of paradise:
- *Alfred Russel Wallace: A Life*, 161-162.

Illnesses from arsenic-treated wood:
- *Is Arsenic an Aphrodisiac?* 69-73.

Neki maha means "crazy ground":
- *Conservation Is Our Government*, 82-83.

PAGE 101

Wallace makes a profit off his birds:
- *Alfred Russel Wallace: A Life*, 161-162.
- *Alfred Russel Wallace, My Life*, 376.

Grandville wrote his own epitaph; his family destroyed his drawings:
- *A Human Comedy*, 102.
- *Public and Private Life of Animals*, intro. by Edward Lucie-Smith, vii.

Benjamin crossing the Pyrenees; he died of inexperience:
- Lisa Fittko, "The Story of Old Benjamin," *Arcades Project*, 950.
- *Illuminations*, 6-7.
- *Walter Benjamin: A Biography*, 261.

Fifty-six new species in Papua New Guinea:
- "New Species Discovered in Papua New Guinea," *The Guardian*, March 25, 2009. Accessed April 23, 2018. http://www.guardian.co.uk/environment/gallery/2009/mar/25/papua-new-guinea-new-species?picture=345036514.
- Kristen Gelineau, "Scientists find new species in Papua New Guinea," AP foreign, March 26, 2009.

SELECTED BIBLIOGRAPHY

Anderson, Terry L., ed. *Property Rights and Indian Economies*. Lanham, MD: Rowan & Littlefield Publishers, Inc., 1992.

Applegate, Debby. *The Most Famous Man in America: The Biography of Henry Ward Beecher*. New York: Doubleday, 2006.

Appel, Toby A. *The Cuvier-Geoffroy Debate: French Biology in the Decades before Darwin*. Oxford: Oxford University Press, 1987.

Arbor, Agnes. "Goethe's Botany." *Chronica Botanica* Vol. 10, No. 2 (Summer, 1946).

Balzac, Honoré de. *Old Goriot*. Translated by M.A. Crawford. London: Penguin, 1951.

Banner, Stuart. *How the Indians Lost Their Land: Law and Power on the Frontier*. Cambridge: The Belknap Press of Harvard University Press, 2005.

Barr, Daniel P., ed. *The Boundaries Between Us: Natives and Newcomers Along the Frontiers Of the Old Northwest Territory, 1750-1850*. Kent, Ohio: Kent State University Press, 2006.

Basbanes, Nicholas A. *A Gentle Madness: Bibliophiles, Bibliomanes, and the Eternal Passion for Books*. New York: Macmillan, 1999.

Beecher, Henry Ward. *Star Papers; or, Experiences of Art and Nature*. New York: J.B. Ford and Company, 1873.

Benjamin, Walter. *The Arcades Project*. Translated by Howard Eiland and Kevin McLaughlin. Cambridge, MA: The Belknap Press of Harvard University Press, 1999.

——*A Berlin Childhood around 1900*. Translated Howard Eiland. Cambridge, MA: The Belknap Press of Harvard University Press, 2006.

——*Illuminations: Essays and Reflections*. Translated by Harry Zohn. New York: Harcourt Brace Jovanovich, Inc., 1968.

——The Paris of the Second Empire in Baudelaire." *Selected Writings*, Vol. 4 1938–1940. Cambridge, MA: Harvard University Press, 2003.

Bortoft, Henri. *The Wholeness of Nature: Goethe's Way Toward a Science of Conscious Participation in Nature*. Hudson, NY: Lindisfarne Books, 1996.

Boyd, Barbara Weidon. "Celabitur Auctor: The crisis of authority and narrative patterning in Ovid Fasti 5," *Phoenix*, Vol. 54, No. 1/2 (Spring-Summer 2000).

Brodersen, Momme. *Walter Benjamin: A Biography*. Translated by Malcom R. Green and Ingrida Ligers. New York: Verso, 1996.

Brosco, Jeffrey. "The Early History of the Infant Mortality Rate in America: A Reflection Upon the Past and a Prophecy of the Future," *Pediatrics*, Vol. 103, No. 2 (February 1999).

Brown, Lee Rust. *The Emerson Museum: Practical Romanticism and the Pursuit of the Whole*. Cambridge, MA: Harvard University Press, 1997.

Buck-Morss, Susan. *The Dialectics of Seeing: Walter Benjamin and the Arcades Project*. Cambridge, MA: MIT Press, 1989.

Burney, Ian. *Poison, Detection, and the Victorian Imagination*. Manchester: Manchester University Press, 2006.

Burrows, Edwin G. and Mike Wallace. *Gotham: A History of New York to 1898*. New York: Oxford University Press, 1999.

Burrus, Virginia. *"Begotten Not Made": Conceiving Manhood in Late Antiquity*. Stanford: Stanford University Press, 2000.

Burt, Richard and John Michael Archer, eds. *Enclosure Acts: Sexuality, Property, and Culture in Early Modern England*. Ithaca, NY: Cornell University Press, 1994.

Canup, John. *Out of the Wilderness: The Emergence of an American Identity in Colonial New England*. Middletown, CT: Wesleyan University Press, 1990.

Chudacoff, Howard P. and Judith E. Smith. *The Evolution of American Urban Society*. Upper Saddle River, NJ: Prentice Hall, 2000.

Cleaveland, Nehemiah. *An Address Delivered Before the New-England Society of Brooklyn, N.Y., December 21, 1849*. New York: The Society, 1850.

——*An Address Delivered at Topsfield in Massachusetts, August 28, 1850: The Two Hundredth Anniversary of the Incorporation of the Town*. New York: Pudney & Russell, 1851.

——*The First Century of Dummer Academy, A Historical Discourse Delivered at Newbury, Byfield Parish, August 12, 1863*. Boston: Nichols & Noyes, 1865.

——*Green-Wood Cemetery: A History of the Institution from 1838 to 1864*. New York: Anderson & Archer, 1866.

——*Green-Wood: A Directory for Visitors*. New York: Pudney & Russell, 1857.

——*A Hand-book for Green-Wood*. New York: E.B. Tripp, 1878.

———*Hints Concerning Green-Wood, its Monuments and Improvements*. New York: Pudney & Russell, 1853.

———*A History of Bowdoin College, with biographical sketches of its graduates, from 1806 to 1879, inclusive* edited and completed by Alpheus Spring Packard. Boston: J.R. Osgood & Co., 1882.

Cohen, Alicia. *Debts and Obligations*. Oakland: O Books, 2008.

Corbey, Raymond. *The Metaphysics of Apes: Negotiating the Animal-Human Boundary*. Cambridge: Cambridge University Press, 2005.

Crawford, Rachel. *Poetry, Enclosure, and the Vernacular Landscape 1700-1830*. Cambridge: Cambridge University Press, 2002.

Cullen, William R. *Is Arsenic an Aphrodisiac? The Sociochemistry of an Element*. London: The Royal Society of Chemistry, 2008.

Curl, James Stevens. *The Victorian Celebration of Death*. Detroit: The Partridge Press, 1972.

Darragh, Tina. *opposable dumbs*. Greenbelt, MD: self published, 2007.

de Tocqueville, Alexis. *Democracy in America*. Translated by Arthur Goldhammer. New York: Literary Classics of the United States, Inc., 2004.

Delbanco, Andrew. *The Puritan Ordeal*. Cambridge, MA: Harvard University Press, 1989.

Dickman, Howard and Ellen Paul Frankel, eds. *Liberty, Property, and the Foundations of the American Constitution*. Albany: State University of New York Press, 1989.

Doughty, Robin W. *Feather Fashions and Bird Preservation: A Study in Nature Protection*. Berkeley: University of California Press, 1975.

Douglass, David Bates. *Exposition of the Plan and Objects of the Green-Wood Cemetery, an Incorporated Trust Chartered by the Legislature of the State of New York*. New York: Narine & Co., 1839, reprinted by Green-Wood Cemetery, Brooklyn, NY, 2006.

Downing, A.J. *A Treatise on the Theory and Practice of Landscape Gardening, Adapted to North America*. New York: Riker, Thorne & Co., Sixth Edition, 1859.

Dunbar, Willis Frederick and George S. May. *Michigan: A history of the Wolverine State*. Grand Rapids, MI: Wm. B. Eerdmans Publishing Co., 1995.

Dunning, Joan. *Secrets of the Nest: The Family Life of North American Birds*. Boston: Houghton Mifflin Company, 1994.

edwards, kari. *bharat jiva*. Brooklyn: Venn Diagram Productions, 2009.

Eliot, T.S. *Four Quartets*. San Diego: Harvest/HBJ, 1971.

Emerson, Ralph Waldo. *The Complete Works of Ralph Waldo Emerson*. Vol 1. Nature, Addresses and Lectures. New York: Houghton Mifflin, 1903, available online at the Ralph Waldo Emerson Institute Digital Archive: http://www.rwe.org.

——*The Ralph Waldo Emerson Journals*, Vol. 3, 1833-1835. London: Constable, 1914, available online at: http://www.rwe.org.

——*The Ralph Waldo Emerson Journals*, Vol. 7, 1845-1848. London: Constable, 1910, available online at: http://www.rwe.org.

Farber, Paul Lawrence. *Finding Order in Nature: The Naturalist Tradition from Linnaeus to E. O. Wilson*. Baltimore: The Johns Hopkins University Press, 2000.

Federici, Silvia. *Caliban and the Witch: Women, the Body and Primitive Accumulation*. Brooklyn: Autonomedia, 2004.

Feld, Steven. *Sound and Sentiment: Birds, Weeping, Poetics, and Song in Kaluli Expression*, Second Edition. Philadelphia: University of Pennsylvania Press, 1982.

Foust, Graham. *Necessary Stranger*. Chicago: Flood Editions, 2007.

Freese, Barbara. *Coal: a Human History*. Cambridge, MA: Perseus Publishing, 2003.

Galdikas, Biruté M.F. *Reflections of Eden: My Years with the Orangutans of Borneo*. Boston: Little, Brown and Co. 1995.

Gascoigne, Ingrid. *Papua New Guinea*. Tarrytown, New York: Marshall Cavendish, 1998.

Getty, Clive F. "Grandville: Opposition Caricature and Political Harassment," *Print Collector's Newsletter* Vol. XIV, No. 6 (Jan-Feb. 1984).

Gillispie, Charles Coulston. *Science and Polity in France: The Revolutionary and Napoleonic Years*. Princeton: Princeton University Press, 2004.

Goethe, Johann Wolfgang von. *Goethe's Collected Works, Vol. 12, Scientific Studies*. Translated by Douglas Miller. Princeton: Princeton University Press, 1994.

Goldberger, Paul. *Up from Zero, Politics, Architecture, and the Rebuilding of New York*. New York: Random House, 2004.

Gotti, Maurizio. *The Language of Thieves and Vagabonds: 17th and 18th Century Canting Lexicography in England*. Tubingen: Max Niemeyer Verlag, 1999.

Grandville, J.J., Taxile DeLord, and Alphonse Carr. *The Flowers Personified*. Translated by Nehemiah Cleaveland. New York: R. Martin, 1859.

——*Public and Private Life of Animals*. London: Paddington Press, 1977.

——*Un Autre Monde*. Paris: H. Fournier, 1844.

Guest, Barbara. *Selected Poems*. Los Angeles: Sun & Moon Press, 1995.

Haraway, Donna. *Primate Visions: Gender, Race, and Nature in the World of Modern Science*. New York: Routledge, 1989.

Harvey, David. *Paris, Capital of Modernity*. New York: Routledge, 2006.

Hejinian, Lyn. *The Language of Inquiry*. Berkeley: University of California Press, 2000.

Holst-Warhaft, Gail. *Dangerous Voices: Women's Laments and Greek Literature*. London: Routledge, 1995.

Howe, Susan. *The Birth-mark: Unsettling the wilderness in American literary history*. Hanover, NH: Wesleyan University Press, 1993.

Hughes, Richard A. *Lament, Death, and Destiny*. New York: Peter Lang, 2004.

Hurt, R. Douglas. *The Ohio Frontier: Crucible of the Old Northwest, 1720-1830*. Bloomington: Indiana University Press, 1996.

Jackson-Houlston, Caroline. "'Queen Lilies'? The Interpenetration of Scientific, Religious and Gender Discourses in Victorian Representations of Plants," *Journal of Victorian Culture*, Vol. 11, No. 1 (Spring 2006) 87-96.

Jardine, N., J.A. Secord, and E.C. Spary, eds. *Cultures of Natural History*. Cambridge: Cambridge University Press, 1996.

Jones, Colin. *Paris, the Biography of a City*. New York: Viking, 2005.

Karr, Alphonse. *The Ladies' Botany* in *The Flowers Personified*. Translated by Nehemiah Cleaveland. New York: R. Martin, 1859.

Keeney, Elizabeth B. *The Botanizers: Amateur Scientists in Nineteenth-Century America*. Chapel Hill: The University of North Carolina Press, 1992.

Kenney, Elise K. and John M. Merriman. *The Pear: French Graphic Arts in the Golden Age of Caricature*. South Hadley, MA: Mt. Holyoke College Art Museum, 1991.

Koeppel, Gerard T. *Water for Gotham: A History*. Princeton: Princeton University Press, 2001.

Lees, Andrew and Lynn Hollen Lees, *Cities and the Making of Modern Europe, 1750-1914*. Cambridge: Cambridge University Press, 2007.

Little, Elbert L. *National Audubon Society Field Guide to North American Trees, Eastern Region*. New York: Alfred A. Knopf, 1980.

Logan, William Bryant. *Oak, the Frame of Civilization*. New York: W.W. Norton & Co. Inc., 2005.

Mails, Thomas E. *Sundancing: The Great Sioux Piercing Ritual*. Tulsa: Council Oaks Books, 1978.

Mann, Charles C. *1491: New Revelations of the Americas Before Columbus*. New York: Alfred A. Knopf, 2005.

McDonald, Forrest. *Novus Ordo Seclorum: The Intellectual Origins of the Constitution*. Lawrence, KS: University Press of Kansas, 1985.

McMullan, John L. *The Canting Crew: London's Criminal Underworld 1550-1700.* New Brunswick, NJ: Rutgers University Press, 1984.

Meckel, Richard A. *Save the Babies: American Public Health Reform and the Prevention of Infant Mortality, 1850-1929.* Baltimore: The Johns Hopkins University Press, 1990.

Mingay, G.E. *Parliamentary Enclosure in England: an Introduction to its Causes, Incidence, and Impact, 1750-1850.* New York: Addison Wesley Longman, 1997.

Mitchell, John Hanson. *Trespassing: an inquiry into the private ownership of land.* Reading, MA: Addison-Wesley, 1998.

Morowitz, Harold J. *Entropy and the Magic Flute.* Oxford: Oxford University Press, 1993.

Nash, Roderick. *Wilderness and the American Mind.* New Haven: Yale University Press, 1967.

Nedelsky, Jennifer. *Private Property and the Limits of American Constitutionalism.* Chicago: University of Chicago Press, 1990.

Neeson, J.M. *Commoners: Common Right, Enclosure and Social Change in England, 1700-1820.* Cambridge: Cambridge University Press, 1993.

Nelitz, Marc, et al., *Managing Pacific Salmon for Ecosystem Values: Ecosystem Indicators and the Wild Salmon Policy.* Vancouver, BC: Pacific Fisheries Resource Conservation Council, 2006.

Nobel, Philip. *Sixteen Acres: Architecture and the Outrageous Struggle for the Future of Ground Zero.* New York: Metropolitan Books, 2005.

Norwood, Vera. *Made from this Earth: American Women and Nature.* Chapel Hill: University of North Carolina Press, 1993.

Notley, Alice. *Desamere.* Berkeley: O Books, 1995.

Outram, Dorinda. *Georges Cuvier: Vocation, Science and Authority in Post-Revolutionary France.* Manchester: Manchester University Press, 1984.

Pipes, Richard. *Property and Freedom.* New York: Alfred A. Knopf, 1999.

Preston, Samuel H. and Michael R. Haines. *Fatal Years: Child Mortality in Late Nineteenth-Century America.* Princeton: Princeton University Press, 1991.

Raby, Peter. *Alfred Russel Wallace: A Life.* Princeton: Princeton University Press, 2001.

Richardson, Robert D., Jr. *Emerson: The Mind on Fire.* Berkeley: University of California Press, 1995.

Richman, Jeffrey I. *Brooklyn's Green-Wood Cemetery: New York's Buried Treasure.* Brooklyn: The Green-Wood Cemetery, 1998.

Robertson, Lisa. *Occasional Work and Seven Walks from the Office for Soft Architecture.* Astoria, OR: Clear Cut Press, 2003.

Rogers, Elizabeth Barlow. *Landscape Design: A Cultural and Architectural History.* New York: Harry N. Abrams, Inc., 2001.

Schama, Simon. *Landscape and Memory.* New York: Alfred A. Knopf, 1995.

Schieffelin, Edward L. and Robert Crittenden, eds. *Like People You See in a Dream: First Contact in Six Papuan Societies.* Stanford: Stanford University Press, 1991.

Seamon, David and Arthur Zajonc, eds. *Goethe's Way of Science: A Phenomenology of Nature.* Albany: State University of New York Press, 1998.

Shively, Charles. *A History of the Conception of Death in America*, 1650-1860. New York & London: Garland Publishing, Inc., 1988.

Siegan, Bernard H. *Property Rights from Magna Carta to the Fourteenth Amendment.* New Brunswick & London: Transaction Publishers, 2001.

Smith, Neil. *Uneven Development: Nature, Capital, and the Production of Space.* Athens, GA: University of Georgia Press, 1990.

Sobelman, 'Annah. *The Tulip Sacrament.* Hanover, NH: University Press of New England, 1995.

Sterling, Eleanor Jane, Martha Maud Hurley, and Le Duc Minh. *Vietnam: A Natural History.* New Haven: Yale University Press, 2006.

Swadling, Pamela. *Plumes from paradise: trade cycles in outer Southeast Asia and their impact on New Guinea and nearby islands until 1920.* Boroko, Papua New Guinea: Papua New Guinea National Museum, 1996.

Takaki, Ronald T. *Iron Cages: Race and Culture in 19th-Century America.* Seattle: University of Washington Press, 1979.

Trilling, James. *Ornament: A Modern Perspective.* Seattle: University of Washington Press, 2003.

Tudge, Colin. *The Tree: A Natural History of What Trees Are, How They Live, and Why They Matter.* New York: Three Rivers Press, 2005.

Wallace, Alfred Russel. *The Malay Archipelago.* Singapore: Periplus Editions, 2002.

——*Infinite Tropics: An Alfred Russel Wallace Anthology*, ed. Andrew Berry. London: Verso, 2003.

——*My Life: A Record of Events and Opinions*, Vol. 1. New York: Dodd, Mead & Company, 1905.

Ward, Diane. *Film-Yoked Scrim.* Queens, NY: Factory School Books, 2006.

Wechsler, Judith. *A Human Comedy: Physiognomy and Caricature in 19th Century Paris.* Chicago: The University of Chicago Press, 1982.

West, Paige. *Conservation is Our Government Now: The Politics of Ecology in Papua New Guinea*. Durham, NC: Duke University Press, 2006.

White, Terence Hanbury and Kenneth Frazier. *The book of beasts: being a translation from a Latin bestiary of the twelfth century*. Madison: The University of Wisconsin Madison Libraries Parallel Press, 1960.

Wilcove, David. *The Condor's Shadow*. New York: W.H. Freeman and Company, 1999.

Williams, Johannes. *Paris, Capital of Europe: from the Revolution to the Belle Epoque*. Translated by Eveline L. Kanes. New York: Holmes & Meier, 1997.

Williams, Michael. *Americans and Their Forests*. Cambridge: Cambridge University Press, 1992.

Wilson, James. *The Earth Shall Weep: A History of Native America*. New York: Grove Press, 1998.

Whitman, Walt. *The Collected Writings of Walt Whitman*, Vol. 1 1834-1846, ed. Herbert Bergman. New York: Peter Lang, 1998.

——*The Collected Writings of Walt Whitman*, Vol. 2 1846-1848, ed. Herbert Bergman. New York: Peter Lang, 2003.

——*Notebooks and Unpublished Prose Manuscripts*, Volume IV: Notes, ed. Edward F. Grier. New York: New York University Press, 1984.

——*Whitman: Poetry and Prose*. New York: Literary Classics of the United States, Inc., 1996.

Wick, Peter A. *The Court of Flora*. New York: George Braziller, 1981.

Wollen, Peter. "The Concept of fashion in the Arcades Project," *Boundary 2, an international journal of literature and culture*, Vol. 30, No. 1 (Spring 2003). Durham, NC: Duke University Press.

Wood, Gordon S. *The Creation of the American Republic 1776-1787*. Chapel Hill: University of North Carolina Press, 1998.

ACKNOWLEDGMENTS

Portions of *Green-Wood* appeared in the following magazines: *Peaches & Bats*; *Magazine Cypress*, *Aufgabe*, *EOAGH*, and *Practice: New Writing + Art*. Thank you to the editors.

This book is dedicated to my loved ones—in poetry and in life—who have given me so many gifts.

I am grateful to the New York Foundation for the Arts for a fellowship that enabled the completion of this book.

ALLISON COBB is the author of *Born2, Plastic: an autobi-ography*, and *After We All Died*, which was a finalist for the National Poetry Series and Oregon Book Award. She works for the Environmental Defense Fund and lives in Portland, Oregon.

NIGHTBOAT BOOKS

Nightboat Books, a nonprofit organization, seeks to develop audiences for writers whose work resists convention and transcends boundaries. We publish books rich with poignancy, intelligence, and risk. Please visit our website, www.nightboat.org, to learn about our titles and how you can support our future publications.

The following individuals have supported the publication of this book. We thank them for their generosity and commitment to the mission of Nightboat Books:

Kazim Ali
Anonymous
Photios Giovanis
Elenor & Thomas Kovachevich
Elizabeth Motika
Leslie Scalapino - O Books Fund
Benjamin Taylor
Jerrie Whitfield and Richard Motika

In addition, this book has been made possible, in part, by grants from the New York State Council on the Arts Literature Program.